EXCERPTS FROM COUNTRY SERMONS

R ev. Bergland was going home after the meal and Pa went out to the car with him. A big old rooster was strutting around there, and the preacher said something to my dad about that "proud old rooster." My dad said, "He ought to be – he's got two sons in the ministry."

❖

S uddenly Rev. Thompson said, in a loud voice: "Andrew, would you please keep those boys quiet. They are disturbing our service with their noise!" I was instantly jolted from fabulous social interaction to a sense of guilt over committing a grievous sin. The spiritual crisis was expanded when I began to wonder what Dad would do after the service."

❖

T his was the first Sundance held by the Sicangu since the Sundance was declared illegal. The first women who came out to dance are called Sundance Mothers. In this renewed beginning, only one Sundance song was remembered and that one song was sung that entire day. Yet, the spirit of that one song joined with the sky and the earth, and with each sacred direction, to bring to us hope.

❖

I t was a pleasant service sequence, and as Lillian and I left, I felt charmed by my first experience in this quaint little country church. It somehow exuded an air of serenity, acceptance, and privacy, standing as it did amid large fields of shining green corn.

COUNTRY CONGREGATIONS

South Dakota Stories

Edited by
Charles L. Woodard

South Dakota Humanities Foundation
Brookings, South Dakota

Library of Congress Cataloging in Publication Data

Woodard, Charles L.
South Dakota Stories

Charles L. Woodard
1. Churches—South Dakota—History
2. Education—Midwest—Memoirs
0-9632157-6-0

© Copyright 2002 by South Dakota Humanities Council
Box 7050, University Station, Brookings, SD 57007
All rights reserved.

First Edition
Manufactured in the United States of America
by Mailway Printers
Composition by Media One, Inc., Sioux Falls, SD

ACKNOWLEDGMENTS

The South Dakota Humanities Foundation Board is very appreciative of the text contributions and the technical and research assistance of the following: Darla Bielfeldt, Duane Bohn, Tiffanny Bolle, Phyllis Boyd, Martin Brokenleg, Bessie Brozik, Karol Carr, Jan Cerney, Helen Christenson, Shirley Conraads, Marian Cramer, Sally Crowser, Sherry Larson DeBoer, Luella DeJong, Vine Deloria, Jr., Valerie Dombrowski, Jon Drew, Darlene Droz, Rebecca Dunn, Shirley Armfield Farrell, Faulk County Lutheran Brotherhood–Branch 8729, John Fiksdal, Darlene Finney, Jim Gederos, Mary Gederos, Rev. Rodney Gist, Gladys Hagny, Christine Halverson, Carol Hansen, Shirley Hansen, Doris Hanson, Miriam Hardy,

Michael Haug, Gladys Hawk, Linda Hipps, Highland Lutheran Church Senior Members, Lucille Houda, Fr. Fred Jessett, Marvin Johnson, Norma Johnson, Ron Johnson, Myra Kalb, Rev. Carl Kline, Barbara Knight, Joyce Knock, Marilyn Kratz, Darrell Lambert, Gerald Lange, Carol Larson, Denise LaRue, Alma Lau, Marvin Lau, Lester Lauritzen, Lanniko Lee, Kermit Liebing, Ardelle Lundeen, Pearl Lundquist, Betty Lusk, Jeanne Jones Manzer, James Marten, Patricia McCreary, Media One, Alice Mentzel, John Miller, Missouri River Lutheran Brotherhood–Branch 8604, Carolyn Mollers, Ollie Napesni, Donald Nemer, Jane Pierce, Joyce Poppen, Rosemary Quigley, Gail Ramynke, Evie Rice, Duane Sander, Donald Simmons, Linda Skadeland, Charlotte Smidt, Orville Smidt, Vance Sneve, Virginia Driving Hawk Sneve, Mauriece Southwick, Naomi Stapleton, Jack Stengel, Patricia Stofft, Arvella Stokke, Helen Svaren, Linda Svoboda, Maxine Swanson, Arvel Trapp, United Methodist Church of Iona History, Herb Uttecht, Janett Uttecht, Violet Van Deest, Audrae Visser, George West, Lydia Whirlwind Soldier, Tolstoy Diamond Jubilee Text, Terry Whiting, Willow Lake Fourth Grade (1999/2000), Ken Wise, Andrea, Laura, and Sarah Woodard.

CONTENTS

Introduction   xi
Charles L. Woodard

Prelude   xvi
Lanniko L. Lee

1. Foundations   1
Audrae Visser, Vine Deloria, Jr., Duane Sander, Shirley Armfield Farrell, Vine Deloria, Jr.

2. Front & Centered   8
Gail Ramynke, Alice Stegeman Mentzel, Martin Brokenleg, Helen J. Svaren, Marvin and Alma Lau and Herb and Janett Uttecht, Lucille Houda, Carol Danielson Larson, Marvin and Alma Lau and Herb and Janett Uttecht, Marian Cramer, Lawrence Welk, Vance M. Sneve, Marvin A. Johnson, Ken Wise, Darlene Droz, Ardelle Lundeen, Marvin A. Johnson, George Augustine West

3. Joyful Noise   26
Marvin and Alma Lau and Herb and Janett Uttecht, Ken Wise, Helen Christenson, Pearl Lundquist, Ronald Johnson, Orv Smidt, Patricia McCreary, Charlotte Lee Smidt, Carol Danielson Larson, Ron Johnson, Father Fred Jessett

4. Come & Get It   37
Joyce Poppen, Carol M. Hansen, Darrell R. Lambert, Audrae Visser

5. The Force of Habit   43
Darrell R. Lambert, Rev. Carl Kline, Joyce Poppen, Linda Johnson Skadeland

6. The Next Generation   49
Shirley Hansen, Norma Johnson, Gail Ramynke, Lester Russell Lauritzen, Phyllis Waldow Boyd, Mary Fulwider, Shirley Reiners Conraads, Marvin A. Johnson, Orv Smidt, Marilyn Kratz, Joyce Knock, Carol Danielson Larson, Virginia Driving Hawk Sneve, James Marten, Rebecca Dunn, Jim Gederos, Darla Bielfeldt, Marvin A. Johnson

7. That Time of the Year   81
Gladys Hawk, Jane Pierce, Joyce Poppen, Violet Van Deest, Luella DeJong, Arvel Trapp, James Marten, Highland Lutheran Church Senior Members, Pearl Lundquist, Marian Cramer, Myra D. Kalb, Norma Johnson, James Marten, Doris Hanson, Ollie Napesni, Naomi Stapleton, Sally M. Crowser

8. For the Good of the Cause   101
Kermit Liebing, Orv Smidt, Duane Bohn, Gail Ramynke, Doris Hanson

9. Uninvited Guests   105
Shirley Hansen, Darlene Finney, Duane Bohn, Joyce Poppen, Father Fred Jessett

10. Outside Interests   109
Maxine Hansen Swanson, Carol M. Hansen, Arvel Trapp, Carol M. Hansen

11. Tests of Faith   113
Darlene Droz, Vine Deloria, Jr., Helen Christenson, Arvella Stokke, Mauriece Southwick, Rev. Rod Gist, Willow Lake 4th Grade Class/1999-2000

12. For Richer, For Poorer   122
Pearl Lundquist, Shirley Reiners Conraads, Sherry Larson DeBoer, Helen Christenson, Miriam Loken Hardy, Alice Stegeman Mentzel, Gladys Hagny, Valerie Dombrowski

13. Coming Forward   130
Lucille Houda, Helen J. Svaren, Marilyn Kratz, Rebecca Dunn, Evie L. Rice, Bessie Brozik, Rev. Carl Kline, Father Fred Jessett

14. What Was Is   139
Lydia Whirlwind Soldier

15. Becoming History   143
James Marten, Marvin and Alma Lau and Herb and Janett Uttecht, Marvin A. Johnson, Jan Brozik Cerney

16. A Meaningful Goodbye   147
Linda Hipps

INTRODUCTION

CALL IT THE ROMANCE OF THE RURAL. Americans have always had an affection for "out of the way" places, landscapes and locales which are mostly free of the clutter and encroachments of that which we call "civilization."

There are consequent ironies. One has been the relentless displacement of the original inhabitants of this land, the native peoples for whom "earth" and "us" are synonymous, for whom the earth itself is sacred text.

Another irony is summarized by the essayist Joseph Meeker, who points out that "the movers and builders" among us must "scramble continually to revamp our surroundings in search of a solution to a problem which is a result of their own activity." Clearly, in the Euro-American history of this country, great emphasis has been placed upon the development of resources and the manipulation of place in the name of progress.

Historically, Americans have had a mostly uncritical view of the word "progress." But in recent years, as the effects of transforming country into city and suburb have become more apparent, many people have become increasingly concerned about the changes, about landscape becoming manscape, and therefore have become increasingly nostalgic about the mostly rural settings of the past, and more drawn to the rural settings of the present.

Nowhere is this nostalgia, this romance of the rural, more obvious than in our long-term enthusiasm for the country church. One of the most popular American songs of all time, "The Church in the Wildwood," by William S. Pitts, begins with this verse:

> There's a church in the valley by the wildwood,
> No lovelier place in the dale;
> No spot is so dear to my childhood
> As the little brown church in the vale.

There is a compounding of the rural and the "out of the way" in these famous lines: this earth-colored little church is set in a picturesque valley near an even more natural place, a wooded area, a forest, a "wildwood."

An unobtrusive little building tucked into natural landscape, what many people refer to as "God's creation," this image of the rural church actually contrasts with the physical reality of many of the early pioneer church buildings. As Robert C. Ostergren points out, what he calls the "immigrant church" was often "the dominant structure on the landscape," rivaled only by the grain elevator. "With its white clapboard siding and gleaming spire," Ostergren says, "it was visible for miles." But even such churches, of course, are small and rural in contrast to the towering assertiveness, the monumental vertical sweep, of many of the city and suburb churches which large numbers of Americans now attend.

INTRODUCTION

An additional appeal of the idea of the rural church, in this time of burgeoning population and accelerated pace, is the lifestyle it models, the lifestyle of small local community, people "congregating" in intimate, mutually supportive ways. Against the facelessness and anonymity of much of urban life and the lonely-in-a-crowd irony, there is the comforting rural church idea of ongoing, meaningful connection and relationship.

This social affection for and nostalgia about the rural country church has many parallels, among the most notable being those with many people's feelings about the rural school, which was the focus of the South Dakota Humanities Council's 1998 publication, ***One-Room Country School***. For that reason, and because the Council is especially interested in the expression and preservation of this region's cultural heritage, this book was conceived of as a companion volume to that earlier publication.

Like the first volume, this publication features as its main ingredient anecdotes, little stories which are emblems of hopes, beliefs, values, possibilities. There is also history here, and a roughly historical sequence in the arrangement of the chapters, but even a summary of the richly varied and diverse spiritual experiences of this landscape is beyond the scope of this book. Many separate volumes detail the various religious traditions represented here, and numerous histories of individual churches are also available.

Also, no attempts were made beyond the general call for submissions to equally represent or even include all of the numerous Christian denominations of this region. Again, that would have been beyond the scope of this project, and also, many of the stories which are included here are broadly representative of most of those denominations.

An effort was made, however, to solicit and include the perspectives and stories of the tribal descendants of the original inhabitants of this area. This effort was made to ensure that this text reflects the multicultural history of this area. It was also made to demonstrate the extent to which tribal perspectives have been and continue to be influential within Christian traditions, and the extent to which the traditional tribal religion has persisted here. The former is evident in the contributions of Vine Deloria, Jr., Virginia Driving Hawk Sneve, Violet Van Deest, Gladys Hawk, and Father Fred Jessett, and the energy and vitality of the latter tradition is evoked especially by Lanniko Lee's Prelude, and by the essays of Ollie Napesni and Lydia Whirlwind Soldier.

There are of course significant differences between the region's main religious traditions. For example, for many years, the sacred tribal circles have contrasted absolutely with the linear configurations of the Christian traditions, with their rows of pews facing religious leaders. However, more recently, some of the Christian denominations have created semi-circle and even full circle physical arrangements for their services, and there seems to be more interest among non-Indians now in having weddings and other special services in outdoor settings. These changes also seem consistent with an ecumenical trend which has become more inclusive in recent years.

This book's cover decisions were also made based on its multicultural emphasis. Congregations are gatherings of people, usually for spiritual purposes, and the "Congregations" of the title refers to all of this area's circles of belief, the oldest of which have been residential here for hundreds and perhaps thousands of years.

This book's cover imagery was chosen to be reflective of both religious diversity and relationship. The Christian and tribal religious objects and configurations can be thought of as separate, the preference of many people, and they can be thought of as combined, the preference of many others. In any case, the total picture dramatizes the importance of that which has not always been a reality in an America proud of its "freedom of religion:" tolerance and mutual respect.

INTRODUCTION

A final word about the title: "Country" refers both to the isolated places of worship on rural landscapes which have motivated most of these stories and to the places of worship within rural communities, the village and towns which are also represented here. Listed with the author's name after each story is the name of the congregation in which the story occurred and the small town or rural place of that story.

As was the case with ***One-Room Country School***, this book is intended to entertain and inform, and to stimulate further research and discussion and storytelling. Again, making selections for this project was difficult, and we are appreciative of all of the interesting and informative materials which were sent to us.

- Charles L. Woodard

PRELUDE

I GUESS I WAS NINE OR SO when I first noticed that my Lakota grandmother spent much of her day singing on her little place on the Cheyenne River Sioux Reservation along the Missouri River.

She always sang as she worked. In fact, seldom did a day go by when she was not singing as she went about making bread or sweeping her kitchen floor or cutting out quilt pieces on the white iron bed in her bedroom. She knew a lot of songs—church hymns, mourning songs, songs of her friends and family, even waltz melodies. She sang songs I knew, but more often she sang songs of her own creation with melodies and words unfamiliar to me and maybe new to her.

Hers was a melodic voice, sweet and light with an amazing range of surprises. I was always amused by what she could make it do.

If Grandma wasn't working and singing, she would rest in her old walnut-colored glider in the backyard—the one with Auntie Amy's worn-out corduroy crazy quilt that hung over the back—and play her mouth harp or harmonica. She knew how to make the harmonica talk and even sound like a woman crying or laughing. I loved to hear my grandmother express herself in music.

"Why are you always making music?" I asked my grandmother one day.

"Well, I guess it's my way of feeling alive," she answered.

Since I knew my grandmother had suffered many hardships over the years, it seemed very strange that someone who had experienced the heartaches that she had would still have it in her to always be deeply immersed in song or whistling or mouthing a melody.

"Do you like to sing?" I asked her.

"Oh, yes." she answered. "We all need to sing. Singing keeps me connected to everything. It's a good kind of water to quench a different kind of thirst."

"You mean singing keeps us healthy?" I asked.

"Yes," she said. "But singing does more than that."

"What's that?" I asked.

"I'm singing and while I'm singing, I'm hoping to sing the one song that the Creator can hear," she said.

Lanniko L. Lee, Java

Foundations

ONE HOT SUNDAY MORNING IN JULY, Lillian Sellevold, a neighbor and good friend of my late mother's, stopped in to see me. I was not surprised, because her husband Obert had died and Lillian undoubtedly was lonely.

"C'mon, Audrae! Pull your nose out of that science magazine and go to church with me!" she said.

"But, Lillian," I protested, "I didn't bother to roll my hair in curlers last night."

"Lone Rock Church doesn't expect women to come looking like movie stars!" she replied. "Comb your hair and let's go!"

Lone Rock Church stood several miles south and east of Flandreau. I had never been in a country church before, so I felt that this would be a good opportunity to become acquainted with one.

Down the road we went. Although the air was drowsy with the scent of yellow sweet clover, Lillian kept me awake with anecdotes about the Norwegian pioneers who had built Lone Rock Church.

At last we arrived. I felt impressed with the neatness of the church and grounds. Evergreen trees surrounded the building on three sides. It was painted a flawless white, and the lawn looked so green and cool that one felt tempted to flop down and roll on it. Evidently, the pioneers' descendants still took loving care of Lone Rock Church.

Lillian and I went up wooden steps to be greeted by a friendly Scandinavian (I assumed that he was Scandinavian because his "s's" sounded like delicate little hisses, just as Lillian's did!).

The church was very small but it had an ornately carved big white altar, a throne-like preacher's chair, and an old piano opposite that. The walls were decorated with felt banners and embroidered religious mottoes.

The room smelled faintly of Johnson's lemon furniture wax. Because all the windows were open, a slight new breeze made us feel fairly comfortable, despite the warmth of the day.

I glanced around, but did not see anybody I knew until I looked at the person sitting on my left. Oh, joy! She was Margaret Brekke, a poet I knew but seldom saw. We whispered excitedly until the bell rang.

The clergyman, who also was the main preacher in the Flandreau Norwegian Lutheran Church, came in wearing his robes, and the congregation sang some hymns. Luckily, there were enough men present to make the singing sound "balanced." A teen-aged girl played the piano.

It was a pleasant service sequence, and as Lillian and I left, I felt charmed by my first experience in this quaint little country church. It somehow exuded an air of serenity, acceptance, and privacy, standing as it did amid large fields of shining green corn.

Audrae Visser,
Lone Rock Church, Rural Flandreau

IN 1912, THERE WAS RIGOROUS COMPETITION between LaCreek and Martin for the county seat of Lugenbach (later Bennett) County. A number of families had moved into LaCreek anticipating that it would be named the county seat. Pete Skalinder had even built a large house that he hoped would be purchased for the offices for the county. But the land was very swampy and infested with mosquitoes and other summer-time pests and roads were nearly impassable during the spring rains. Also, LaCreek was not centrally located, whereas Martin was almost dead center for county residents.

The supporters for a county seat in LaCreek had been so optimistic, however, that they had built an Episcopal church before the election for the county seat occurred. Raising $1,000 themselves, which was a near impossibility in a land with few settlers and even less hard cash, they encouraged Bishop Hare to match their money, and Grace Church was built. The cemetery for LaCreek is just south of the church about thirty yards, and many original settlers, regardless of church affiliation, are buried there.

But then, of course, the county seat designation went to Martin. As LaCreek dwindled and then vanished, with buildings being moved to Martin and Tuthill, the church fell into disrepair and the harsh Dakota winters took their toll. People were scrambling to find work, and while many families continued to live in the vicinity, the fathers and older children were often away from home doing odd jobs to keep their families and homesteads intact.

Aside from Christmas, the big celebration at Grace Church was the annual Memorial Day service and the cleaning of the cemetery. The grass was burned off, weeds were cut, and graves were carefully raked and cleaned. New markers were put up as necessary. Families gathered to instruct the younger children about the names on the gravestones, bringing to life people who had passed on before their births.

In 1936, after cleaning the graveyard, the people began walking back to the church to have lunch and the difference between the now immaculate graveyard and the church struck them hard. After a delicious potluck lunch, the people held a meeting to discuss what to do about the church.

That fall after the harvest was done, the people returned to LaCreek with tools, paint and building materials. In an afternoon, the old building was transformed into a clean, modern church gleaming with new paint, a restored belfry, and new front steps. Now it looked so good that Grace Church began a Sunday school during the school year and hosted a Vacation Bible School for many years, until World War II scattered the families.

Vine Deloria, Jr.,
Grace Church, LaCreek

YOU MIGHT WONDER WHERE the architectural design of many country churches originated. When Jim and Betty Lusk of Brookings toured Norway in 1997, they visited the church where Betty's relatives worshiped, the Briem Church near Reed, Norway.

To their surprise, the church was similar in design to the Belleview Lutheran Church north of Howard, my former church. It is their understanding that the design of the Belleview Lutheran Church was greatly influenced by the design of the church in Norway, because Betty's ancestors, who moved to South Dakota from Norway, wanted to worship in a church similar to their childhood church.

The members of the local Ladies Aid, who wanted a place to meet, originally requested the Belleview Lutheran Church. It was built in 1886 on six acres of donated land that would accommodate the church, a horse barn and a cemetery. Services and Ladies Aid meetings were held in individual homes until the church was built. The church building cost a total of $1,462.88. The bell, donated by the Luther League, has the inscription "My tongue shall speak of thy praise."

The outside structures and the inside appearances of the Briem and Belleview churches are very similar. Each church has a main sanctuary and a steeple construction that also provides an entry area to the sanctuary. Each church has an intricately carved altar, a circular communion rail, and seating for the pastor and assistants.

Duane Sander,
Belleview Lutheran Church, Rural Howard

ABOUT THE TIME WE WERE READY for a permanent church, the Fort Randall Dam in Pickstown was under construction and my brother, Rolland Armfield, was working for a contractor on that project. One week before the dam was to be finished and the area flooded with water, a large grove of red cedar trees in the lowlands was auctioned and Rolland bid on and acquired a section of that grove. He then notified the men of our church, and a group of them went to work cutting down those trees and hauling them out of there. The Andersons had a sawmill at Butte, Nebraska, and they cut those trees into lumber, with which the men built the church on the state line, just ¼ mile east of the little town of Jamison, Nebraska.

The result was a beautiful little church with the complete interior in natural finished red cedar, including the pews. This all occurred during corn-picking season, but willing men gave up their time, and many of their sons handled the corn crops while their fathers were building our church, on land donated by Ed Prchal.

Shirley Armfield Farrell,
Jamison Full Gospel Church, Rural Jamison, Nebraska

IN THE MIDST OF THE GREAT DROUGHT of the 1930's, some of the Sioux people on the Pine Ridge reservation took things into their own hands. Remembering that Eagle Nest Butte near Wanblee, South Dakota, had been the site of frequent vision quests in the old days, they decided to build a small temporary church on top of it so that they could pray for rain. Robert Two Elk, Fred Twin, and Jake Hawk, prominent Episcopalians who attended Gethsemane Chapel in Wanblee, petitioned Bishop Roberts to come to the butte and hold special prayers for rain.

The service was held in front of a large cross that had been erected by the three men. A pine bough booth was built annually to house the clergy and other dignitaries during the service. People came from all over the Pine Ridge and Rosebud reservations and camped there for several days, visiting, enjoying social gatherings, and saying some special prayers for their families and communities.

The most important service was held on Sunday morning and everyone wore his or her finest clothes for this service. The prayers were for rain, and fertility of the soil, and for the animals, domestic and wild, which were suffering in the drought. Then Holy Communion was held. Finally, many people walked around the sides of the butte, placing flowers and tobacco sacks with their prayers.

This special annual service was begun in 1936 and continued until 1943, when war-time gas rationing prevented the bishop from attending, as he lived in Sioux Falls and could not travel long distances. When queried about the effectiveness of the services, some old-timers swore that more often than not, they got rain as they were leaving for home.

Vine Deloria, Jr.,
Eagle Nest Butte Church, Rural Wanblee

Front & Centered

I HAVE VERY WARM MEMORIES of Peever Lutheran Church from my childhood. Peever was part of a four-point parish. The other three churches served by our pastor were rural churches located in the foothills of the Coteau de Prairie. It was quite a feat for the pastor to conduct four separate services driving between churches every Sunday morning. On weeks when ours was the first service of the day, instead of greeting the parishioners on the step after the service, the pastor would swiftly proceed down the aisle during the closing hymn with his vestments flowing, and down the steps to his waiting car to "gun it," in order to make it to the next church before the end of their opening hymn.

Gail Ramynke,
Peever Lutheran Church

REV. F. W. LEYHE, UPON HIS GRADUATION from the seminary in St. Louis in June, 1895, accepted a call to St. John's Lutheran Church of Wolsey. A native of Grand Rapids, Wisconsin, and used to that wooded country, he could hardly fathom the endless prairies of South Dakota on his way to Wolsey by train.

Rev. Leyhe was to serve at Yale, Onida, Cavour, Highmore, and Blunt as mission stations. During his first year, he traveled 6,432 miles by horse and buggy. He traveled by horse and buggy for 22 years. Onida was 90 miles from Wolsey, Blunt was 70 miles, and Highmore 50 miles. His salary was to be $150 per year at Wolsey and the same at Yale; the first six months he received $14 at Wolsey and $18 at Yale. The congregations at Blunt, Highmore and Onida paid him in meat, bread, and canned goods.

During his second winter, he had to leave his team at Yale until spring, after the first snowfall of 18 inches on October 23. The snow was six feet on the level that winter and no one could make it to services, so Rev. Leyhe went back to Wisconsin for a spell.

In setting up housekeeping, Rev. Leyhe sent to T.M. Roberts Co. for three chairs at $.41 each, a table for $.98, and, for a few dollars, a set of dishes and a frying pan. When the order came, he didn't have money enough to pay the freight, so he had to wait and save for some time.

He slept on a buffalo robe on the floor with a quilt for a cover. He was used to this, because wherever he stayed, the homes usually had no extra beds, and in his writings he said that he slept very well.

He stated that he knew the ladies by their hats when he preached his sermons, as he could not see their faces.

"There were no marriageable daughters at Wolsey that could cook, sew on buttons, bake, wash, and darn socks, only 13 lonely bachelors," he wrote. He returned to Wisconsin in 1898 to meet a girl his sisters had selected for him, and she met with his approval. After some correspondence, he returned to marry her in July of that same year.

Alice M. Stegeman Mentzel,
St. John's Lutheran Church, Wolsey

IN THE 1870'S, THE FEDERAL GOVERNMENT assigned the Episcopal Church to be the official mission church to the Lakota people and then added the Catholic Church to the mission's assignment as well.

These two churches, which were the only denominations permitted on the reservations in those days, have always had good working relationships. Years ago, they even had joint masses. At a joint service, a priest of each denomination would stand at the altar and they would take turns speaking each section of the service.

My father, a long-time Episcopal priest, often took part in these joint masses with his friends among the Catholic clergy. At the offertory, the priests from the two churches would set out bread and wine side by side. When it was time for Communion, congregants from both churches would go forward from whichever side they were sitting on.

At one mass, it happened that all of the Catholic nuns came to my father's side of the altar to take Communion. Later, they were questioned about this by the Catholic priest. "Sisters, why did you take Communion on Father Brokenleg's side today?" the priest asked. After a pause, one sister said: "Well, frankly, Father, he has better wine."

Martin Brokenleg
Professor, Native American Studies, Augustana College

PASTORS' WIVES WERE AMONG the unsung heroes in the early days. Many of them had musical talents. Parishioners would volunteer to sit by the pastor's children during worship to free their mother to accompany hymns on the organ. Other wives assisted by directing choirs or leading the Sunday school music. Also, because some churches saved money by heating their buildings only on weekends, the pastors' wives were hostesses of many mid-week meetings in the parsonages.

Pastors' wives also served as Sunday school teachers, vacation church school instructors, Bible study leaders, counselors, and advisors to women's groups. All in all, these women were invaluable in helping their husbands fulfill their callings.

Helen J. Svaren,
Trinity Lutheran Church, Arlington

COUNTRY CONGREGATIONS

IN THE EARLIER DAYS, there were two large heat registers on the floor in the front of the church. Before the service, men of the congregation often visited in the furnace room in the basement. One Sunday morning, one member was talking rather loudly right below the register, shortly before it was time for the bell to ring. Pastor Haase, who valued silent meditation before services, walked over to the register and loudly stamped his feet on it. "SILENCE!" he said. Coming upstairs, the man who had been talking slid into the bench and said to a fellow worshiper: "Wer hat das geton?" ("Who did that?")

Marvin and Alma Lau,
Herb and Janett Uttecht,
St. Peter Lutheran Church, Rural Armour

ONE OF THE EARLY PRIESTS in our church kept demanding money. The people had so little that they would often bring him food instead. Still, he kept demanding money, and his demands became irritating.

Then one day a parishioner sold him a horse that was considered to be a "lemon." The reverend hitched the horse to a buggy and gave him a swat and the horse didn't move. So the reverend got down and swatted the horse across the rump with his cap. The horse took off and kept going, leaving the reverend seething and parishioners standing nearby trying to suppress their laughter.

That priest didn't stay very long, and soon another priest drove out from Kimball to serve our church. This one was a very good man, and dearly loved.

Lucille Houda,
Holy Trinity Church, Bendon
(relocated to Kimball, 1982)

My minister father had enough interesting experiences to have written a book, but we children knew little of that side of his ministry. In his retirement he occasionally shared some of the more memorable ones. His view from the pulpit was elevated and sometimes people weren't aware of that.

He recalled that once in the middle of his sermon, he looked down and saw a young couple in the back row who had forgotten where they were, as the young man was caressing his girlfriend's breasts. I think he recalled that he completely lost his train of thought and had to recover himself the best he could and go on and try to ignore the back row!

Carol Danielson Larson,
Sun Prairie Baptist Church, Rural Salem

Upon coming home from a full Saturday morning of confirmation instruction under Pastor Heber, one of the young boys was helping his father with the horses, which weren't being very cooperative. The father was becoming exasperated and used a swear word on the horses in German. The boy said to his father, "Today Pastor taught us that we are not supposed to swear." The father replied, "Pastor doesn't have to work with horses!"

Marvin and Alma Lau,
Herb and Janett Uttecht,
St. Peter Lutheran Church, Rural Armour

IT WASN'T AN ORDINARY SUNDAY MORNING. The cows were milked, and we had breakfast; that part was usual. My older brothers were staying home to take care of things and do the rest of the chores and they would milk the cows again in the evening. Mother had put a tea towel inside a clean bushel basket as a liner and filled the basket with picnic fare we would eat and share this day of camp meeting. Mom and Dad and my sister and I were in our Sunday best as we climbed into the car and headed down the road towards town. We drove right through Frankfort and on towards Redfield. Our Frankfort Methodist Church was not having services so everyone could go to the Beaulah Park Camp Meeting.

As we turned by the Wilson motor court and headed down the street toward Turtle Creek, we entered a green woods. A few years later I would learn the song, "My Green Cathedral." The campgrounds of Beaulah Park seemed to me like a green cathedral, with the tall trees spreading their limbs covered with green leaves to form a canopy. Beneath the tall trees, the building that was lovingly called a tabernacle sat like a gray hen with wings that could be spread to shelter the worshipers. The wings were actually the sides of the building that could be raised and held up by poles. In the heart of the tabernacle, it was always dusty on the plank seats. The dirt floor was covered with clean straw. My sister and I hoped our folks would choose to sit near the lifted up sides. They usually did, and toward the front, so they could hear well and be near the open sides so a little breeze might come in. It was usually quite warm in late June.

That Sunday, the Sunday I remember best, I was ten and my sister was six. We were seated on the planks and the service began. Our Frankfort pastor was on the stage with some other area pastors, but there was a visiting pastor named Pastor Robinson who was the main speaker for the day and his skin was not white. In the center of South Dakota in the early 1940's, I had seen one or two Native Americans, but never a person with black skin. My father smiled his gold tooth grin at me and said, "Pastor Robinson is a child of God. We'll do well to listen to him." He patted my shoulder and I knew things would be as they should be.

One of the local pastors led the invocation. Another led the responsive reading, and yet another did the Bible reading for the day. Then Pastor Robinson stepped forward. It seemed to me he looked at everyone in the large congregation personally. I was certain he had looked right into my soul. I was sitting straight and tall and listening carefully. Pastor Robinson spoke with a deep, mellow, voice. "Brothers and Sisters, are you hurting? Are you worried about our young serving our country?" Then he nodded to the pianist, who had a good command of her instrument. She played some mellow chords and Pastor Robinson sang. It was not an ordinary voice, for it seemed to fill the tabernacle and drift out the sides to rise to the tops of the trees. "There is a balm in Gilead...to cleanse the sin-sick soul...there is a balm in Gilead to make the spirit whole."

When he finished the song, the congregation was silent. Even the chirping birds near the open sides had hushed their singing. Then Pastor Robinson spoke to each of the people in the tabernacle. He soothed their spirits; he set their worries at rest for a time and he covered the congregation with a cloak of God's love. His closing line was "Rest in the Lord...Rest in the Lord."

Then he stepped back to his chair and the men's quartet from the Tulare church gathered at the front and sang: "I come to the garden alone, while the dew is still on the roses, and the voice I hear, falling on my ear, the Son of God discloses..."

Then another pastor stepped to the pulpit and said: "Brother Robinson will lead the services at 2:00 and at 6:30 this evening. (Almost the entire congregation returned for both services.) Let us join in Hymn 82, "We're marching to Zion!"

"Come ye that love the Lord and let your joy be known. Join in the song with sweet accord, join in the song with sweet accord, and thus surround the throne. And thus surround the throne. We're marching to Zion, beautiful, beautiful, Zion, we're marching onward to Zion, the beautiful city of God."

Beaulah Park is gone, though Turtle Creek still runs through the wooded area near Redfield. Still, in memory, I return to Camp Meeting again and again. The promise of that special Beaulah Park Camp Meeting remains in my heart.

Marian Cramer,
Frankfort Methodist Church

I CAN'T HONESTLY TELL YOU I remember sitting forlornly on the steps of the Tolstoy Town Hall, but I can tell you Tolstoy wasn't the only town that had mixed feelings about dancing back in those early years.

My little band and I were playing for a typical Saturday night dance. We had a big turnout and everyone was having a good time. When it came time for "Goodnight Ladies," the dancers took up a collection and asked us to keep playing a little longer, and the hat got passed around again and we played "Just a Little Longer" again and again.

I was feeling pretty good about our great success when I went to mass Sunday morning—until I found myself the subject of the sermon. The subject was "The Devil Who Came to Town." I didn't feel so good after that, and learned to be somewhat cautious about letting Saturday night fun spill onto Sunday morning!

Incidentally, the good Father did forgive me in time. It wasn't long before we were invited back to play for a dance sponsored by the church.

Musically Yours,
Lawrence Welk
(Reprinted from the **Tolstoy Diamond Jubilee** *book)*

NORWEGIAN WAS THE CODE LANGUAGE used by my parents to communicate information not intended for my ears. Not so with my oldest brother and my elder sister, both of whom spoke fluent Norwegian and had to brush up on their English skills before starting grade school. To them, Norwegian Lutheran was not just the name of a religion, but also an extension of their Norwegian heritage. They memorized the Norwegian catechism and understood sermons in Norwegian as well as those in English.

Pastor Kildahl was the minister for our Lake Campbell congregation, but he lived in the parsonage at Volga where his primary church was located. He had probably delivered Norwegian sermons in the past, but times were slowly changing, and when I was growing up, he used English in his services. He was an older man who always wore a black suit that hung loosely on his tall frame. He never expressed any emotion in his demeanor or in his sermon delivery, but neither did most of us other Norwegians.

Some of the congregation thought he was cold and aloof, but we never got to know him beyond the pulpit. At the last minute, he would speed into the churchyard, and run in the door behind the altar, where he robed and rushed into the sanctuary to conduct the service. After the service, he immediately exited through the same door and rushed off to the congregation waiting in Volga.

The only time we saw Pastor Kildahl outside of the church was at the annual Sunday school picnic. I remember I saw him slip away from the gathering at one of the picnics and light up a cigarette. It was not a pipe or a pinch of snuff like Norwegian men used, but a more evil Hollywood kind of cigarette! I was disillusioned to catch him in what was probably his only vice. However, I've reflected on this over the years, and I'm sure that St. Peter never gave it a thought when Pastor Kildahl approached the Pearly Gates.

Pastor Kildahl's church services were dull and uninteresting to a young boy, but when we had visiting pastors, they were even more tediously boring. Visiting ministers were often missionaries returning from Madagascar. My mental vision of Madagascar was that of half-naked head-hunting natives being preached at by these men of the cloth, who urged them to mend their ways. The sermons these visitors gave didn't offer much clarification, since they were delivered in the dreaded code language—Norwegian!

Sometimes I think of going to Madagascar to set my mind at ease concerning several unanswered questions. Such as: 1. Is Norwegian the primary language in Madagascar? 2. Do the Lutheran converts in Madagascar send missionaries to other countries? 3. Do the natives still keep shrunken heads, and are any of them from Norwegian Lutheran missionaries?

Then again, perhaps I don't want to know the answers, as they might destroy my vivid memories of growing up Norwegian Lutheran.

Vance M. Sneve,
Lake Campbell Church, Rural Brookings

COUNTRY CONGREGATIONS

My father was a committed lay minister of the small non-denominational church in Bijou Hills. He served the church for about 45 years, and, since his retirement and death, the church has closed and fallen into disrepair. Dad's zeal for the ministry included "street meetings" in town on Saturday nights during the summer. With loudspeaker in hand, he would admonish passers-by to become better Christians or "repent and change your ways."

As a small boy, I was terribly conflicted about those meetings. I was expected to go and I did enjoy being with Dad and the couple who usually played guitar and sang. The conflict was between several sets of priorities. I felt I should be at the meetings and visible at all times, for Dad's sake. I also feared that God would be displeased if I was not actively participating. But I also wanted to walk the streets, visit with my cousins, buy popcorn from the street vendor, and have fun!

To add to my dilemma, sometimes Dad would call on me for a "word of testimony." This would usually happen if some children stopped to listen. His asking was always unexpected, and I never knew quite what to say. I was very shy and lived in fear of his request. So I made a plan. I would stand very visible for a time, then sneak off for a quick walk, and then stand visible again as if I had never left. That worked so well that I once sneaked into the town movie theatre and saw part of a war movie. Since movies were "forbidden," this was an incredibly bold step!

However, the small town grapevine worked fast and on my way home Dad said, "How did you spend your time in town?" "Just walking around," said I. "I heard you were at the movie." "No," I shouted with a guilty voice, "who told you that?" That was the end of the conversation. We rode in silence the rest of the way home. We both knew the truth!

As I got a bit older, and understood more, I learned to appreciate that aspect of Dad's ministry. Lives of many people were touched. Some got more interested in their spiritual lives, and a few began to attend church. I admired the commitment that it took for Dad to conduct those meetings, as many people did not want to be bothered and showed those feelings in various subtle ways. The lessons I learned about commitment to a cause, about sharing your feelings with others, about beliefs, about not reacting to negative criticism, and about doing what you think is right, are still ingrained in me, 60 years later.

Marvin A. Johnson,
Bijou Hills Church

REV. BERGLAND SERVED THREE CHURCHES: Revillo, Big Stone and Alban. Alban was his last service of the day. As we went out the door, everybody shook hands with him. He would say, "Mary? (That's my mother) You got anything to eat out at your house today?" He would go someplace to eat every Sunday. One day on the way home, Ma said to us kids: "Now I killed only two of those leghorn roosters, so you kids wait—take a wing or something." So we kids were pretty careful. Later, when Rev. Bergland was going home after the meal, Pa went out to the car with him like he always did. A big old rooster was strutting around there, and the preacher said something to my dad about that "proud old rooster." My dad said, "He ought to be—he's got two sons in the ministry."

Ken Wise,
Alban Evangelical Church

THE SON OF THE PASTOR who served from 1914 to 1918 recalls that on a trip to Miller by horse and buggy, his father had to open two gates. The pastor left his sons by the cracker barrel at the store while he did the shopping.

This pastor liked to tell the story about a couple who were not getting along very well. The woman told the Reverend as they watched a team and wagon go through the streets that she wished she and her husband could pull together like that team did. The husband's comment was:

"We could if there was only one tongue between us."

Darlene Droz,
Pleasant Valley Community Church, Rural Miller

FOR ALL OF MY CHILDHOOD YEARS, our church functioned under the dictatorial reign of a strict monsignor. "Rigid" was probably an understated description of the good man.

Nuns were the teachers in our parochial school and they were expected to discipline the students not only in school, but also in church. All children were to sit in the front pews in ascending order of age from front to rear, closely monitored by the nuns, who were not averse to pulling ears if children got noisy or started to giggle, especially during a lengthy sermon by the monsignor. One of the final prayers was "Thanks be to God." This usually elicited a too-loud "Amen" from the students and warning looks from the nuns.

One incident stands out in my mind after half a century. My parents always went to the 6 a.m. Mass and, of course, took me with them. They also always sat very near to the back of the church. One Sunday morning, Monsignor came through the back door, saw me, grabbed me by the ear and marched me to the front of the church, even though there were no nuns there at early Mass.

My father was sputtering, but there was nothing he could do. No one could argue with the monsignor.

While we may have thought our monsignor was one-of-a-kind, I imagine that he was more typical than atypical of that era.

> Ardelle Lundeen,
> St. Lawrence Catholic Church, Milbank

THE SQUARE, WHITE, wood frame church at Bijou Hills had been given up by the Methodists and sold to the congregation in the early 1900's. The community had become so small that it could not support a full-time clergyman. It sat empty until my father, as a lay minister, began to serve the church about 1941. For almost 45 years, he drove 30 miles each way on Sundays to minister to the small but dedicated group of members. Since his retirement and death, the church has been unused and is in progressing stages of decay and disrepair.

My dad never expected to be a minister. He didn't finish high school, and married just before the Depression. I came on the scene during those early, horribly difficult Depression years. He and mother struggled to make a living on the farm, as they watched grasshoppers ruin crop after crop. The dust and dryness stunted whatever crops the grasshoppers left, and survival was almost impossible. Dad also worked for the WPA, repairing local gravel roads, and we accepted dried foods from government agencies.

In 1940, a traveling evangelist named Ole Barnes came to our small country church and made a tremendous impact. Our church had "revival meetings" about once a year, usually in the fall. I was only nine years old, but I remember him and his message well. He was probably in his 60s, short and stocky, somewhat balding, with a powerful and persuasive voice. At one of the evening services, with voice rising and trembling with emotion, he pleaded with and cajoled the small congregation. "Any of you knows not of tomorrow—you may die and be lost forever," he said. "Tonight may be your last chance to repent and turn to God. Jesus is calling; don't turn Him away."

Then the congregation sang softly the old hymns "Just As I Am" and "Almost Persuaded." The evangelist asked us to bow our heads as we were singing "with no one looking up," as he asked for raised hands of those who wanted prayer. Then he invited anyone to "come forward to the altar for salvation." The church had a small kneeling area covered with worn green velvet around the pulpit, and soon it had several people kneeling, all tearful, all responding to the message of the evangelist. The small group included Mom and Dad.

From that point on, my father was a changed man. He began to read and study the Bible with diligence. Every morning, I would hear him praying out loud, in his upstairs bedroom, for guidance and direction. He began to teach adult Sunday school and, in 1943, he was asked to become the minister of the small Bijou Hills Church, which he did. About 45 years later, having rarely missed a Sunday, he retired and the church closed its doors for good.

The interior is now stripped, its white siding missing in places and worn away to a dull grey. Its windows have been broken, and birds and small animals make it their home. But it stands as a monument, at least to me, of a man who in one evening changed his whole perspective on life. He then devoted the rest of his days to this new vision, purpose and direction, which had a profound effect not only on his life but also on the lives of his family and on the whole community.

Marvin A. Johnson,
Bijou Hills Church

MY PARENTS LOVED Father George Augustine Esterguard, their parish priest in Big Stone City, and I became one of his favorites during my youth. He served at St. Charles Parish for over 25 years, until he was asked by the bishop to move to Dell Rapids to help them build a new church. That was in 1950; I was just entering seminary, to explore the possibility of becoming a priest myself. I visited Father Esterguard in Dell Rapids for a couple of weeks in the summer of 1951. The new church and rectory were complete enough that I stayed in a guest room in the new rectory. Father looked tired and old beyond his years (he was only 54 then), but we had a good visit, attending some movies and baseball games. He so hoped that I would continue on in the seminary and one day take his place.

Father died suddenly that autumn of 1951. After attending the funeral, I never went through Dell Rapids again. Father George and everyone in Big Stone City had always planned for him to be buried in Big Stone City, but, since he died as pastor of St. Mary's in Dell Rapids, he was buried in the cemetery there.

I continued at the seminary for four more years, but gradually came to realize that the priesthood was not for me and left. My life took a wandering path through various jobs, the Army, marriage, and college, until I moved to Brookings in 1969 to join the faculty of the English Department at South Dakota State University. I still frequently thought of Father George, and sometimes felt as if I had let him down, since I had never had the chance to discuss my decision with him.

I must have driven to Sioux Falls dozens of times over the years without ever having to go on old Highway 77 through Dell Rapids, since the interstate now went by the town three miles to the west. In 1988, I drove to Sioux Falls yet again to take my wife Wanda for a medical appointment. Wanda and I started back to Brookings that afternoon, relieved at a favorable diagnosis. As we neared the Dell Rapids exit, I told her that I just had gotten a sudden and strong urge to visit Father's grave, and that I had to find it.

We drove into Dell Rapids and then to the cemetery, where I found the grave rather quickly. I stood looking down at the stone inscribed with "Please Pray for Me." As I finished my prayer and turned back to the car, I suddenly felt that everything was just fine in my world, that perhaps Father and I had just had our discussion after all. As I slid into the car seat I said to Wanda: "I really never knew the date he died; it was October 25, 1951." Completely startled, she said: "Today is October 25th."

George Augustine West,
St. Charles Catholic Church, Big Stone City

Joyful Noise

Across the stillness of the Sabbath morn
The silv'ry church bells call
Sweet their tones, that on the troubled hearts
Like heavn'ly blessings fall.
A holy calm o'er earth is stealing
Tho'ts of joy and blessed peace revealing.
Come and worship while the bells are pealing
Praise the Lord of all.

THE MEN'S CHOIR OF ST. PETER LUTHERAN, which sits in a valley in east-central South Dakota, has often sung this song, "Come and Worship," which was written by Mable K. Rosemon and Ruth Keys Kennerly. The steeple in this church has housed the same bell since 1911, nine years after the church was organized. Until recently, the bell could be heard throughout the countryside one hour before church-time, one-half hour before church, and at the hour church began. Now, the bell is only rung one-half hour before church and at church time.

In the '50s, this heavy bell, which weighs 828 pounds, was tipped over by young Luther Leaguers as they were ringing out the old year and ringing in the New Year. Scared to death, the leaguers reported the tipping of the bell to Emil Fink, expecting to be properly reprimanded for pulling the rope too hard. However, Emil just quietly came to church, climbed up the inside of the tower, and reset the bell. The practice of ringing out the old year and ringing in the New Year has been going on for longer than any of the present members can remember—we have all been part of this. Until the early 1990's, there was a New Year's Eve service at 8 p.m. Following the service, members would gather at a nearby home for refreshments and bonco. At 11:30 a.m., they would file into cars and make their way to church to ring the bell. Before the ringing of the bell, hymns were sung. "A Few More Years Shall Roll" was always a favorite. At exactly midnight, the old year would be rung out, and the bell would be tolled the number of the New Year coming in. The latter practice continues.

This same bell also announces the death of a member to the surrounding neighborhood. The bell tolls the age of the member who has been called home to heaven. Then, at the funeral, as the mourners proceed from the church to the cemetery, the bell tolls until all are gathered at the graveside.

If you drive by St. Peter Lutheran on a Sunday morning and you hear the bell tolled three times, you will know that the congregation is praying the Lord's Prayer. The bell is tolled at the beginning of the prayer, in the middle, and at the end. Recently, a visiting pastor from Germany commended the congregation for continuing this tradition that was begun in Germany, and also for still ringing the bell by hand. A recent addition to the scene is a spotlight, which shines on the steeple that contains the bell and also displays the cross.

Marvin and Alma Lau,
Herb and Janett Uttecht,
St. Peter Lutheran Church, Rural Parkston

THE FAMILIES OF THE CHURCH took turns being janitor. What was the most fun was in the summertime on Sunday morning, when I would go up and dust and sweep a little, and then I got to ring the bell. Now there was a Lutheran church down by the quarry, and they'd ring their bell too, but just a little, and I'd wait until they'd ring their bell and when they got done, I'd ring our bell. That sounded so nice on a summer morning. The air was crisp and the sound carried. That was pretty. I think maybe I rang it a little louder than necessary. We could hear the church bells at the farm more than a mile away.

Ken Wise,
Alban Evangelical Church

I HAVE BEEN A CHURCH PIANIST for over 50 years. In my memories of my home church and other small churches I have known, music is the part of the worship that speaks most strongly to me.

In our Strandburg Baptist Church, one early memory is of my sister, Ruth, two years older than me, being "drafted" to sing in a girl's trio. It was Christmas, and someone on the Sunday School Christmas program committee had decided that the program and the church needed a trio. Ruth sang soprano. My sister-in-law, Violet, sang tenor, and Gertrude Korsberg sang alto. Their first performance must have been a success, as I remember them singing often for Keystone Young People's meetings, for special evangelistic meetings at the church, and on other special occasions. As quickly as one member of the girls' trio would marry and move away, another young girl would be found to replace her, and the music played on. Others who sang in "the trio" were my sister-in-law Anna and I. I do not remember that we sang any special trio music, just familiar hymns.

Finding someone to play for congregational singing was a problem, too. One of the church matrons, Mrs. Dahlberg, solved the problem early in the life of the church by forcing her son, Paul, to take piano lessons from the local teacher, Professor Cesander, until he was ready to "play for the church." Paul became quite a good musician, and played for church for many years, until he married and left Strandburg.

After that, I remember a series of not-as-talented accompanists, and I used to dislike the way one in particular used the piano keys as a drum, I thought. Then Paul Peterson and his wife, Ruby, moved back to Strandburg to settle and raise their family, and the church was blessed with a truly gifted musician, and the town was blessed with a first-rate music teacher. It was Ruby who organized the last girls' trio, made up of her two daughters and Carol Linngren. These three are now grandmothers, but each time we hold a school reunion, a centennial, or any other community-wide event, these three ladies come from their homes in Vermont and Northern Minnesota to sing. They are still simply referred to as "the trio."

Helen Christenson,
Strandburg Baptist Church

A MEMORABLE SUNDAY MORNING SERVICE was during the time when we owned a "pump" organ. The pastor's son had to sit beside it and pump it as his mother, the organist, played. One Sunday, the son fell asleep. Alas, no matter how hard the poor lady played, no music came forth! The boy was soon jolted awake, however, and the service proceeded.

Pearl Lundquist,
Tabor Evangelical Lutheran Church, Strandburg

DURING THE WINTER OF 1880-81, there was a very heavy snowfall. When spring came, the flood came, destroying part of Vermillion. Fred and Pete Heglin salvaged an old organ which was lodged in the driftwood along the river. The owner did not want it, so they took it home and repaired it.

After sitting up a few nights practicing scales and harmonies, Fred Heglin was able to master the notes of the Psalm Book. He became the first regular organist for his congregation. He was given a collection of $5 to $10 every Easter Sunday.

Ronald Johnson,
*Reprinted from **The History of the Dalesburg Evangelical Lutheran Church**, Vermillion*

I REMEMBER A BLACK MEN'S MUSICAL GROUP visiting our church and singing about bones: "them bones, them bones, them dry bones, now hear the Word of the Lord!...the toe bone connected to the foot bone, the foot bone connected to the heel bone...now hear the Word of the Lord!" Wow, could they sing!

Although their enthusiastic singing was rather loud for us Methodists, the congregation was attentive. Maybe we were in shock!

Rep. Orv Smidt,
Sterling Methodist Church, Rural Brookings

Two of the charter members of our church were twins, Erick and Magnus Englund, who had come from Sweden with their wives, children, and other family members. They settled on adjoining farms near LaBolt, and eventually built identical large Victorian homes. They did everything together! They especially liked to sing together, and even sang on the radio.

As their 80th birthday neared, on October 26, 1928, the members of the congregation decided to give them a surprise birthday party to show their esteem and thank them for all they had done for the church.

Two days before their birthday, the twins were told there would be a special speaker at the church that night. When Erick and Magnus and their wives arrived, they were escorted to the front pew. Then the program began. Naturally, music was a big part of it.

First, nine of the Englund's children went to the platform and sang a song to their fathers. Next, passages of scripture were read, talks were given by various luminaries, and telegrams were read from Englund children who lived far away and could not attend. Then there was more music—the church choir, a men's quartet, and a children's choir. And of course, the twins themselves entered into the festivities by singing a duet to the congregation.

After the service, the assemblage moved into the church parlor, which had been decorated for the occasion. There was even an arch of 160 candles, which were lighted in honor of the birthday "boys." Of course, everyone present enjoyed birthday cake and coffee, all being satisfied with their surprise, especially the honorees, who had so often filled our church with song.

Patricia McCreary,
Mission Covenant Church, LaBolt

My grandparents, Henry and Nora DeNeui, celebrated their 50th wedding anniversary in our family church surrounded by family and friends. My dad, Royce Lee, was the emcee that day, and he got more than he bargained for.

One of my grandma's requests for that service was that my cousins Jerelynn and Janice Driessen join with me to sing "Put on Your Old Gray Bonnet." A little nervously, we started singing, and to our horror, one of us started on the wrong note (I think it was me, but everyone was too gracious later to blame me). To the amazement of all, including the three of us, because we were in our 20's and old enough to know better, we then got the giggles. And the more we tried to sing, the worse we got!

Our husbands, sitting together, knew what was coming. I'm told that one of them whispered "Here they go!" And away we went, finally just standing there hanging on each other and laughing until my dad came to the rescue by rising and announcing: "Let's all join in on the chorus!" Then we all sang together: "Put on your old gray bonnet, with the blue ribbons on it, while I hitch old Dobbin to the shay. O'er the fields of clover, we'll ride out to Dover, on our Golden Wedding Day."

Charlotte Lee Smidt,
Evangelical United Brethren Church, Twin Brooks

Growing up in a Swedish Baptist minister's home meant hearing lots of stories about "Good Old Swedes." In fact, I don't remember ever hearing about any other kind. Both my parents spoke Swedish, especially when they didn't want us to know what they were discussing. The "Good Old Swedes" often hadn't mastered the new language completely, so lots of them had trouble with the letter "J," and often pronounced it with a "Y" sound.

With the importance of music in our church, and given the amount of talent in the congregation, it was inevitable that some of the best music came from them. My four sisters and my two brothers and I were always waiting for the male quartet to sing the old favorite, "On the Jericho Road." It came out like this: "On the Yericho road, there's room yust for two, no more and no less, yust Yesus and me." I'm afraid we embarrassed our father with our uncontrollable, stifled giggles. We always got the giggles in church, maybe because we knew we shouldn't.

Carol Danielson Larson,
Sun Prairie Baptist Church, Rural Salem

SHE WAS BORN ON JANUARY 29, 1875, in a simple dwelling on the Dakota prairie, half a mile from the church that her Swedish immigrant parents had helped to build a few years before.

She attended the Dalesburg Country School during the 1880's and later studied music at the University of South Dakota. She became a music teacher—the neighborhood piano teacher.

She was also a homemaker —a single woman living most of her life with another single sister, two single brothers, five nieces and one nephew, Marvin Dahlberg.

She began playing the organ here at church in 1900 at the age of 25. In 1916, she received a new organ to play—a pipe organ made in Pennsylvania, freighted by rail to Centerville and hauled in horse-drawn wagons to the church.

She continued to play the organ, Sunday after Sunday, year after year, decade after decade. She took a leave of absence for one year in 1918. She resigned as organist in 1946, and in the minutes of the Annual Meeting on December 12, 1946, it says:

"It was unanimously voted that Miss Mina Lind, who has been the organist for many years, be elected Organist Emeritis, after she had asked not to be a candidate for the position again." She continued as a substitute organist. Her tenure as organist here at Dalesburg Lutheran approached 50 years.

On August 21, 1952, Mina was canning beans and noticed that her heart was beating fast. She went to bed that evening, never again to have an earthly wakening.

Her funeral was planned for August 26. As the time approached for the service to begin, the electricity went off. There was no electricity to energize the pump that filled the organ wind chest with air to make the organ sound when the keys and pedals were pressed. The organ was silent.

There was no organ music for the woman who had played the organ on the Dakota prairie for over 50 years.

Ron Johnson,
Dalesburg Lutheran Church, Vermillion

OUR LAKOTA CONGREGATION HAD A LAY MINISTER called a helper, a man who had been there for many years. I was priest-in-charge, but he was the real local pastor. His younger brother was a Roman Catholic and when that brother died, I attended the wake and funeral out of respect for the helper.

I'd conducted many wakes and funerals in my years on the reservation, so I was quite used to the keening cries of the women and sometimes the men at the wake and at the cemetery as the grave was being filled. I understood that the mourners were really singing, but I had never been able to hear the words and I admit it sounded like wailing to me.

At his brother's wake, I stood with the helper at the coffin and offered a prayer. Then he touched his brother's body and began his song. By now I knew some Lakota, and this time I heard the words and had an idea of what he was singing. Tears running down his face, his grief clearly evident in his voice, he sang "Mi'Sun, Mi'Sun ("Younger Brother, Younger Brother"). Then he sang of how hard life would be without his brother and of how he would miss him, punctuating his lament with "Mi'Sun, Mi'Sun."

Although I now minister far away from where that beautiful and deeply moving experience occurred, it still always comes to mind when I work with grieving people, trying to help them find ways to express their feelings. There is an old Lakota saying that you must not keep grief inside; you must let it out, or it will make you sick. How much healthier it would be for all of us if we could learn to sing our grief.

Father Fred Jessett,
St. Andrew's Episcopal Church, Spring Creek

Come & Get It

CHURCH PICNICS WITH GATHERINGS that filled the church lawn were held each year, with mission festival being the most attended event. Women accustomed to feeding threshing crews made and brought in potluck dinners. I can still visualize the ample selection of hot dishes and salads, and especially the many tasty desserts. Our country church has no running water, so it is a major project to wash all those dishes at each gathering. Our water is drawn from a hand pump that first has to be primed by pouring water from another source into it. After moving its long handle up and down in rapid succession, water freely pours from its metal spout. Once primed, the pump supplies our water needs for the day.

Of course, it only furnishes cold water, so we must fill and heat big gray graniteware coffee pots on the stove. To conserve the hot water, white metal dishpans are placed inside the deep lengthy old sink, one for washing and another for rinsing. Without plumbing, we use rusty five-gallon pails under our sink drain to catch wastewater. Excitement abounds when someone dumps the dishpan before doing a periodic check to see if the pail below is full, causing a spillover onto the floor with women scurrying to mop it up. For all dinners served, each lady has her given duty of dishing up plates, or pouring coffee, or serving desserts, or washing and drying dishes.

Work never seems like work on these occasions. With all the warm conversations and hearty laughter filling the air, it is more of a celebration. In the history of all the years of potluck dinners, only once did we all bring the same hot dish. Laughter filled the church kitchen as each of us uncovered our dish to discover we all had made calico beans.

Joyce Poppen,
St. John's Lutheran Church, Dempster

MY DADDY WAS THE PASTOR of this little church in the 1950's. It didn't have any amenities except for the outhouse out back.

One weekend, they had scheduled special meetings at the church. The ladies were to serve for an afternoon meeting on Saturday. They decided to serve chicken and noodles, the favorite dish of the guest speaker, Rev. Painter. We had some good cooks who could make delicious chicken and noodles.

After the meeting, everybody who came to the services went downstairs for dinner and bragged about the chicken and noodles, especially the guest speaker, who ate several helpings.

There was an evening service, so the ladies just left the food covered with dishtowels on the table. There wasn't any refrigeration.

Well, don't you know this preacher's daughter sneaked downstairs before the evening service to snitch a piece of cake. I noticed someone had left the lids all ajar on the pans of chicken and noodles. I thought, "That's dumb!" I put them all on tight. I didn't know you shouldn't do that because a gas would form and spoilage would set in.

After church, someone said: "There's lots of food left downstairs; let's go heat it up and have snacks." Rev. Painter and the rest of us ate a lot of chicken and noodles. Gee, they were good!

We then took Rev. Painter and another man home with us to the parsonage to spend the night with our family.

Oh boy. About midnight, we all awoke with cramps and bad diarrhea. We had one bathroom in the old parsonage, and all of us were lined up waiting and sick.

Finally, I couldn't wait any longer. I took off out the door for that outhouse behind the church. It was a block away, but who cared! I was one white streak in a long white nightgown heading for that outhouse. I didn't even bother with shoes and it was November!

Dad went downtown to the drugstore the next morning as soon as it opened and bought the biggest bottle of Pepto Bismol they had. We all survived, no thanks to me! I still like chicken and noodles, but I wonder if the preacher does!

Carol M. Hansen,
Church of God, Gettysburg

I REMEMBER THE ANNUAL ICE CREAM SOCIAL at the Presbyterian Church in Fedora during the 1950's. Members of the church would bring their hand-crank ice cream makers to the church and contribute to the fixings for the event. The young girls of the church would act as waitresses for the evening and serve people sitting at the long tables in the basement. Typically, the girls would take your order and ask: "How many scoops of ice cream would you like?" Most people would respond "one," or "two," and would also select some other dessert that might be offered. My father, Earl Lambert, who was a 4-H leader and a general "flirt" with the church girls, would respond: "How big of a bowl do you have, Sweetie? I want eight scoops of ice cream." He'd then polish those off, and it was not uncommon for him to order another two scoops for good measure. The church girls would "flirt" back with my father, and every year he would order the eight scoops (although I think he later changed his order to "a quart, please"), and the girls would vie to be the waitress to serve the Lambert table! Everyone in the church knew that Earl Lambert would eat the most ice cream at the event.

Darrell R. Lambert,
Endeavor Presbyterian Church, Fedora

SEVERAL YEARS HAD PASSED. The congregation of the Lone Rock Church had grown small, and nobody came anymore on Sunday mornings unless it was a mouse, so they decided to close it.

One day the Moody County Enterprise announced that a reunion and potluck dinner would be held the next Sunday for former members and friends of the Lone Rock Church.

I was not a member, but I felt like attending and asked another friend, Fern Stuefen, if she would like to accompany me. It was a perfect day for church and a potluck dinner and she agreed to go. I took a big bowl of plump green grapes and she took a cake.

Lone Rock Church looked exactly as it did that other Sunday so long ago when I had visited it for the first time. The little white church surrounded by evergreens on an inviting green lawn was still there. Inside, the ornately carved big white altar with the preacher's "throne" and an old piano on either side still stood, and once again the windows were open to let in a refreshing breeze. Once more I was pleased to see my old poet friend, Margaret Brekke, with her new husband, Don Severt, sitting in the back of the church where my friend Lillian and I had sat that Sunday so long ago.

But this time a different preacher greeted us. He was the younger brother of Lillian's husband, Obert. During the service he sang several solos, and his voice was thrilling. Obert had been so proud of his younger brother and wished that he too had become a preacher. "But," said Obert with a sigh, "I wanted to run around and see the world first, so I never got around to learning how to preach. I've always regretted it."

After services, people poured into the church basement with pans of delicious-smelling fried chicken, macaroni and cheese, and many other hot dishes. There were salads galore and ice cream and many cakes for dessert. Soon the long sawhorse tables were lined with former members noisily and merrily exchanging news and jokes as they ate. I looked out over these happy people and thought about what a fine thing many churches do by drawing diverse members together pleasantly with dinners, bazaars, and fund-raisers for good causes. Churches are the glue that hold many small communities together.

The children quickly gobbled down their dinners and headed outdoors to play games of ball and tag. After eating, Fern and I crossed the road in front of the church to enter the cemetery, which also was bordered with evergreens. We read names on the gravestones and saw that almost every surname ended in "sen," as Scandinavian names often do.

We found Lillian's grave and I felt sad to think that she was no longer with us. She and my mother and I used to enjoy discussing books and magazines that we had read. As former schoolteachers, we had a lot in common.

Then it was time to leave and I drove Fern home, glad that we had attended the Lone Rock Church reunion—because at my age, I probably would not get to attend another one.

Audrae Visser,
Lone Rock Church, Rural Flandreau

The Force of Habit

IT'S FUNNY HOW HABITS TURN INTO TRADITIONS. As a very young boy, I noticed that we sat in the same pew every Sunday. Because my father was the "bell ringer," we always had to arrive early—and we always sat in the last pew on the right-hand side of the church. There were three seating sections: the left, the center, and the right. Dad always sat next to the aisle, then Mother sat next to him, and we kids sat to the right of Mother. Sometimes my older brothers sat in front of Mom and Dad. Dad's duties also included passing the offering plate, another reason for him to be at the end of the pew. The young people of the church generally sat in front of the Lamberts, because sometimes one or more would be part of the service sequence, singing or speaking. In the center section, last row, exactly in the center, sat Bob Fox and his mother—every Sunday, every time! Harvey and Arlene Bennett sat right center, second row from the back—every Sunday, every time! The Petersons sat right center, back row—every Sunday, every time! And the Demmings and the Hummels sat—well, you get the picture. It didn't take me long to realize that you could see who was missing at church just by looking at whose "space" was empty!

Darrell R. Lambert,
Endeavor Presbyterian Church, Fedora

IT'S TRADITION IN OUR SMALL CHURCH to recognize birthdays during the announcement time before our Sunday morning service. Once we discover how many years we're celebrating, we sing "Happy Birthday."

Most people are shy about admitting birthdays and having us sing to them. Many try to hide it. It becomes a contest between family members as to who will announce Mom's birthday, or Dad's, or Grandpa's. Usually someone other than the celebrant tells us about it.

I'm no exception as pastor! I also try to avoid the ritual.

One November, on the Sunday before my birthday, I wondered if someone would remember I had a birthday coming up and make the announcement. The time for announcements came and went. No one said anything. Even my wife was quiet. I breathed an inner sigh of relief and gave my wife a grateful smile. I congratulated myself, having sneaked through this part of the service. Still, I knew I wouldn't be home free till the service was over.

Actually, I was looking forward to this birthday. I had become a button collector and was expecting to get some buttons for gifts. If you have ever have an opportunity to see some of the antique clothing buttons I'm talking about, you'll understand. They are made out of so many different materials, by artisans. They are miniature works of art in shell, metal, china, glass, vegetable, ivory, rubber, horn, pewter, silver, etc. You name the material; you'll find a beautiful antique button made out of it.

Our Sunday morning service continued. By the time my sermon was concluded, I had forgotten all about my birthday. We had our pastoral prayer and the ushers came forward and got the offering plates. They passed the plates through the pews as always and came forward as we all sang the doxology. I was ready to say the offertory prayer, when I noticed that the offering plates were filled, not with money, but with buttons. My facial expression must have changed dramatically, because at that moment, the church filled with laughter and the congregation joined with the organ in an upbeat rendition of "Happy Birthday."

I discovered after the service (after we took a second "real" offering), that people in the congregation had been encouraged to bring buttons to church for this surprise birthday gift. What I received was truly a collection from many households. It was a thoughtful and surprising addition to our birthday ritual.

Rev. Carl Kline,
United Church of Christ, Willow Lake

I HAVE ATTENDED THE SAME SMALL CHURCH my entire life. Every Sunday, the Licht family always crowded into my father's Chevrolet for the six-mile ride to church. The car was usually filled with song and laughter. Our family numbered nine: with my parents, Walter and June, my dad's brother, Uncle Mike, and my siblings Patsy, Diana, Paul, Joan, William and me. Now, the rides to church are only three miles, and I travel instead with my husband Lyle and sometimes with our daughter Naomi. Naomi is the fourth generation of my family to attend this small country church. My grandparents, William and Minnie Loats, were members of the church when it reorganized in 1932. My mother and father met at youth group gatherings and remained lifelong members.

Belonging to that country church has taught me many things about life, including "thou shalt not" and "thou shalt," but more importantly, it has taught me life's joys and sorrows and God's unending love.

Also, on the humorous side, it has taught me that every family occupies the same pew each Sunday, and that you never want to accidentally sit in someone else's place. I can still remember which pews were occupied by which families through the years. The sturdy oak benches that lined the left side were filled with the Selcherts, the Janssens, the Loats, the Kiihls, the Temples, the Begalkas, and the Watlands. On the right side sat the Mangels, the Poppens, the Rusts, the Schwankes, the Saathoffs, the Brendens, the Kreuls, the Runges, the Jeffers and the Feldhuses.

My favorite spot on our family pew was next to my father. I would rest my head on his strong shoulders, sometimes struggling to stay awake through the long sermons. Occasionally, I'd feel my father nudge me in an attempt to keep me awake. But when I was a teenager, I was "too grown up" to sit next to my parents. Then my brother Paul and I sat near the back of the church. We promised Dad that he wouldn't hear a peep out of us. We knew where we would be sitting the next Sunday if he did.

The years sped by, and soon our family pew held only my parents and my Uncle Mike. My brothers and sisters all married and moved to new locations and began attending their own churches. While spending a year away at school, I never dreamed that I'd again attend that little country church. Little did I know that God had a plan for me. When our church members started writing letters to members in the military during the Vietnam war, I chose as my correspondent my secret heartthrob, Lyle Poppen. Fortunately, he felt the same way about me as I felt about him.

Through our marriage, Lyle and I became related to almost half of the members of St. John's. With family all around us, we chose a new spot next to my Grandma Loats. Sitting next to Grandma was not always enjoyable, since she sang out of tune, but Lyle and I would smile at each other because we knew, no matter what the sound, that she always sang from her heart.

We were married for five years before our sweet baby Naomi was added to our family pew. She had her great-grandma beside her, her maternal grandparents behind her, her paternal grandparents directly across the aisle, and Lyle's uncles, aunts, and cousins all around her. By now, I no longer wanted to be away from my parents. I loved sitting ahead of my father so I could hear his tenor voice in perfect tune with every note.

That joy turned to sorrow four years later. His sudden death left not only emptiness in the church pew, but an even greater emptiness in our hearts. On that cold January day when my father's bronze-colored casket was wheeled down the church aisle, I learned how much a heart could hurt and yet how much love a church family could supply. At times it's still difficult for me as I sit in my spot and envision my father sitting behind me.

With my father gone, my family sat next to my mom, and my grandma sat in the pew directly ahead of us. Special times followed for all of us as we watched Naomi partake in all the Sunday school programs. The Christmas Eve service was always the most warm and memorable of times. The service was done mostly in song and the church was lighted and decorated. Seeing all the pews filled with family members home for the holidays made for special times. Watching the children perform all dressed in their Christmas attire as they stood fidgeting at the altar always brought soft laughter to the church members. The children, trying hard to concentrate on their scripture verses that told the Christmas story, could not always keep their dancing eyes off the packages beneath the lighted tree.

COUNTRY CONGREGATIONS

If only those joyous times could be our only experiences. Four years after we lost my father, my grandma was gone. Then, just two years after that, Lyle's father was suddenly taken from his place in the church pew. This time, our place didn't change, for Lyle's uncles took turns sitting next to their sister Katie.

Then seven years passed and attendance remained the same for both of our families. Watching the lives of the members unfold brought much happiness. Marriages and crying babies kept the church alive.

The vision of another empty place came with my mother's unexpected surgery just prior to her 65th birthday. For two years after that, which were far too short, we thought of Mom's absence from the pew and from our lives. Then, on an April day, the toll bell rang 67 times. That day, as we sang our final hymns of goodbye to our beloved mother, our family bench, even though full, never felt emptier. Then, only three months to the day and the hour of my mother's death, my uncle Mike's funeral was also held at St. John's. This was the last time my brothers and sisters were all back sitting side by side on those old oak benches we had shared in our youth. I thought this was more than my heart could bear. But once again, His unending love carried me through.

There still are times when tears roll down my cheeks as I sing those familiar hymns, and I sometimes wonder whose spot will be empty next. Time has changed a lot of things at St. John's, and sometimes it's hard to think of the future. As my eyes move around this small country church, the empty places outnumber those that are filled, and I wonder if those pews will ever be filled again.

Many of my memories seem sad, but sadness is an unavoidable part of life. I feel it is better that I was there to experience the joyous times, even though I am also deeply affected by the sorrowful times, than never to have shared our family pew with those I love. At times I picture them all there in their places again, each with his or her special mannerisms. Remembering Lyle's father's slightly altered stride from his farm accident, my grandma's sweet smile, my father's tenor voice, and my mother's gentle presence, all of which still seem so near, fills my life again. And I also remember that true life, the full life we have in Christ, allows us all to live on forever.

Joyce Poppen,
St. John's Lutheran Church, Dempster

ATTENDING A COUNTRY CHURCH in southeastern South Dakota in the 1960's was, for me, as much a part of life as eating and breathing. Besides being a place of learning about God and His Word, the church I grew up in was a sanctuary of stability as solid as the prairie ground upon which it stood.

It never once crossed my young mind that my two sisters and my parents and I would not be there each Sunday in "our" pew—the one on the east side of the center aisle about halfway down. My paternal grandparents would be in "their" pew on the same side of the church, a few rows in front of us. I could count on my dad's aunts and uncles to be nearby in their "assigned" seats, as well. Sometimes one or the other of these great-uncles would catch our girlish eyes during the service and make my sisters and me laugh. The pew would shake as we tried to stifle the giggles and tried not to get "the look" from our parents.

The sense of belonging I felt sitting in that church week after week was absolute. I was surrounded by immediate and extended family members, and I shared Swedish roots with the others in attendance. Adding to this feeling was the knowledge that this very land upon which I sat had belonged to my great-great-grandfather. I had heard the story many times. He had come from Sweden with his wife and children and, upon seeing a need for a church in the community, had helped to establish one.

During recess of summer Bible school, I would steal away from the group and visit the graveyard. I would skip along the winding maze of polished stones and arrive at the most familiar spot. It was as if I knew these great-great-grandparents and great-grandparents who rested there. Their tombstones towered above the ground with my name, "Johnson," carved in bold letters. I would run my hand slowly over those indented letters, then turn and quickly run and play with the other children, whose ancestors were also lying nearby.

The years have come and gone. Now I live in a distant metropolitan area, but the heritage of family and the memories of my South Dakota country church live on in me. Most importantly, my faith is strong today because the seeds of that faith were planted in my heart so many years ago.

Linda Johnson Skadeland,
Benton Lutheran Church, Rural Crooks

The Next Generation

WE REALLY ENJOYED THAT CHURCH. We had lots of get-togethers there. That's about all we did as kids, go to the church. It was Sunday morning and Sunday night, and Wednesday night was prayer meeting and Friday night was young people's night. We'd get together at somebody's house. I remember a sleigh ride party at our house—the kids were all falling off the sleds into the snow.

> Shirley Hansen,
> *Grant Center Evangelical United Brethren Church,*
> *Rural Milbank*

COUNTRY CONGREGATIONS

BETHEL LUTHERAN CHURCH, in Norway Township, Roberts County, was the center of our lives during the 1940's and 1950's.

Norwegian services were still held once a month in the 1940's. Even though everyone spoke the English language, the older people enjoyed having the service in the language of their native country.

Once a month, the Luther Leaguers would meet and put on a program. Everyone came; this was the social event for the month. A lunch was served and I recall looking forward to eating "boughten" white bread sandwiches with dried beef. Some youngsters would even manage to sneak a sugar lump or two out of the white sugar bowl.

Norma Johnson,
Bethel Lutheran Church, Rural Claire City

SUNDAY SCHOOL WAS HELD IN THE CHURCH; all over the church in every nook and cranny. We'd all gather in the sanctuary for opening exercises: a prayer, a song, and recognition of birthdays. The superintendent of the Sunday school had a little bank shaped like a church. Those children and teachers who had birthdays that week were called to the front. The birthday persons would put coins in the bank totaling their ages. Little children would put their pennies in one by one, and invariably an older boy in the back would call out the age of the child. Then everyone would sing "Happy Birthday." Teachers usually preferred to shorten the process by using nickels, dimes and quarters. The boy in the back would faithfully count the clinks and call out the teacher's age as "four" or "seven."

After the opening session, each class went to its respective "room." This might be a corner of the church, a little room behind the altar, or the kitchen in the basement. My favorite "room" was a space behind the piano that made a tiny triangle with the piano positioned diagonally against the corner.

Our church was truly an extended family for me, where the spirit of Christ's welcoming love embraced me throughout my childhood.

Gail Ramynke,
Peever Lutheran Church

I WAS VERY SHY AND BASHFUL as a young boy, a trait of character that adulthood and beginning retirement have only slightly altered. On the Sunday that the beginners' Sunday school class was to start, it had been arranged that two older girl cousins would escort me to class to meet my teacher, which made me feel a little more comfortable.

That first day, our teacher, Clara (Mrs. Peter) Andersen, gave each of us a slip of paper with one of the Ten Commandments written on it, which we were supposed to memorize for the next Sunday. Being kindergarten age, I had not yet learned to read, but I dutifully put my slip of paper in my suit coat pocket, and then either forgot it or ignored it.

This was repeated the next Sunday, and the next, the one I remember the best. When class was dismissed that Sunday, I crossed the street and got into the back seat of the car to wait for my parents, who were visiting with other parishioners. My mother was standing near the car with two other ladies, one of whom was the mother of one of my classmates. As my classmate approached, the child's mother said: "Oh there you are. I suppose you have another commandment to learn?" When my parents came to the car, they asked me about my commandments, and I then produced the three slips of paper from my coat pocket.

I assume that I learned them and the others eventually, but my memory ends in the car that third day of Sunday school. Our family did not have devotions at home. Perhaps if we had, I would have been comfortable enough with religion to have remembered to give those slips of paper to my parents, for them to teach me.

Lester Russell Lauritzen,
Our Saviour's Lutheran Church, Viborg

IT WAS A BEAUTIFUL WARM, SUNNY JULY Sunday morning in 1940. We Sunday school students were gathered in the pews in the front of the church for our opening exercises and our hymn singing, before we were dismissed to go to our classes. The north windows of the church were open to let in a cool breeze on this hot summer day. I was sitting next to my cousin, Marilyn, as we enjoyed our peppy opening songs.

Suddenly there was a loud blast! One of the older boys had tossed a lit firecracker through the open window and it had landed in the pew between my cousin and I—just as it blew!

We were not seriously burned, but it could have been a disaster.

Phyllis Waldow Boyd,
Lake Whitewood Lutheran Church, Kingsbury County

LOIS KENZY AND I WERE IN CHARGE OF THE MUSIC. We had a choir. All of the children could sing. As our families grew larger, so did our choir. We divided the choir into two age groups, the senior choir, which included children in the sixth grade and up, and the junior choir, those younger. As soon as a child could talk and sing, she or he was in the choir. The church ladies made gray gowns with white collars for the seniors, and white capes with red bows for the juniors. The children would sing every Sunday.

We always took the children on a hay ride in the fall. Charlie Thompson would take us in his hay wagon. We would go in different directions, but the children liked best going west and south of Iona as far as the spring in the Sinclair pasture, singing songs as they rode. Some of the boys enjoyed jumping off the wagon and running to climb back on. At the spring, the children would climb banks and trees, and run races and play games. Charlie would build a camp fire and cut green limbs so we could roast hot dogs and marshmallows.

We had other social events in the church basement. The "haunted house" was always fun on Halloween.

At Christmas time, of course, we put on a program. Charlie Thompson was our handy man for that. If we needed a prop, he would make it. One year he made a tree form for the choirs to stand on.

As our children grew older and moved away, our choirs gradually grew smaller. Our last choir consisted of four girls: Claudia Hickey, Jolene Fulwider, and Tammi and Angie Christensen. They sang every Sunday. The song "Love is a Circle" was my favorite.

Mary Fulwider,
*Reprinted from **United Methodist Church of Iona:***
Celebrating 100 Years of Faithfulness

COUNTRY CONGREGATIONS

MY FAMILY AND I ATTENDED a small country church for many years. I was a shy newcomer to our community, and our church was the first social contact I had with our new neighborhood. Our grandmother and our uncle, aunt and cousins already were members of the small congregation, so it seemed appropriate that we should attend the Evangelical Church in the very small town of Twin Brooks. My grandmother soon decided that what she termed the "holy roller" church was not to her liking, so she transferred her membership to the Methodist Church in Milbank. But we remained steadfast members until the church was sold to the Presbyterians and we transferred our membership to the Milbank United Methodist Church.

Looking back after more experiences and with a more worldly perspective, I can see that life was simpler with fewer choices to be made, than is true for my grandchildren today who all attend large, big city churches. We did not wrestle with the issues of drug use, premarital sex, AIDS or divorced parents. We were taught a very definite set of rules to live by, and there were few gray areas in our catechism teachings. There was very little doubt about the consequences of disobeying the "thou shalls" and "thou shalt nots" of the Bible. We were required to memorize many Bible verses, many of which I can remember to this day.

One of the things I vividly remember is learning the books of the Bible and how to find them quickly. We had a drill at the end of every catechism session to find as quickly as possible the book of the Bible which our pastor had asked for. My sister and I were always competing to see who could find the books first. It was usually a dead heat, as I recall. She claims she was faster, but of course I challenge that!

We had an active youth group, led by our young pastor and his wife, who directed us in skits and plays. I even recall my first kiss. The climax of a drama, which we presented, called for the hero (a handsome young man) and the heroine (me, a shy gawky teenager) to kiss. We just faked it during our rehearsals, but the night of the play before a large audience assembled in our town hall, our brave hero did actually kiss me heartily, to the delight of the onlookers. I was not terribly surprised, because I had deduced that he did like me quite a lot. I often wonder if he remembers that night. I think every woman remembers her first kiss!

Shirley Reiners Conraads,
Twin Brooks Evangelical Church

MY GREAT-GRANDFATHER HELPED build the church of my childhood, and my grandparents, parents, and I all faithfully attended. Our church served well the needs of the farm community in both the spiritual and the social realms.

Our family always sat in the same pew. It was on the right side, close to the center, near the pot-bellied wood stove. In mid-winter, I was always hot, as the stove valiantly over-extended itself to heat the building during the below-zero Sundays. It seemed that everyone I knew attended, including our extended family. I couldn't wait to see them all and compare notes about the previous week or share plans for the next.

Sometimes our spiritual and social worlds clashed, as they did one Sunday when I was about eight years old. I left Mom's and Dad's spot to sit with my favorite cousin, Bobby, next to my Grandpa Andrew. It was so wonderful, sitting by Grandpa, with his arm resting on the pew behind us, and talking to my best friend and cousin, Bobby. During the hymns, we couldn't hear to talk, but when the sermon started, we began to whisper furiously. Grandpa said nothing, which was like him. But as the sermon progressed, I guess maybe our whispering got a little too loud and our behavior more animated than it should have.

Suddenly our minister, Rev. Thompson, said, in a loud voice: "Andrew, would you please keep those boys quiet. They are disturbing our service with their noise!" Grandpa kind of nodded in assent but didn't actively restrain us. I was instantly jolted from a fabulous social interaction to a sense of guilt over committing a grievous sin. Disturbing the service! The minister admonishing me! What would God think? Could I be forgiven? I had never heard Rev. Thompson do that before, so I must have really been behaving badly. The spiritual crisis was expanded when I began to wonder what Dad would do after the service. Certainly a talking-to. Maybe a punishment...Were my relatives ashamed?

The worst was that I couldn't discuss any of this with Bobby during the remainder of the service. We didn't dare say another word or look at each other, lest Rev. Thompson would think we were communicating again.

The service ended, and with fear and trepidation, I hesitantly left the church. Bobby sought out his parents, and I slowly also found Mom and Dad. No one said anything! No one mentioned my indiscretion, not even Rev. Thompson. I guess they all thought we had learned a lesson, and had already been punished enough, and they were right!

Marvin A. Johnson,
Trinity Lutheran Church, Rural Platte

MOM ALWAYS DRESSED US IN OUR "Sunday best" for church, and my brothers and I and my parents always sat together in the same pew. Sometimes we would "act up," whispering too loudly or jabbing each other or trying to get Mom to let us play. Then Dad would frown and our parents would sit between us.

One Sunday when I was about three, I was sitting between my older brother Duane and my younger brother Dor and we were a little livelier than usual. The lady sitting behind us, a young recently married farm wife, leaned forward and said to my dad: "Can't you control those boys?" Dad responded: "Just wait until you have kids!"

I believe that she eventually had five, and I'm quite confident that Dad's words came back to haunt her.

Rep. Orv Smidt,
Sterling Methodist Church, Rural Brookings

IN THE SMALL RURAL CHURCH I attended as a child, the pastor preached in "high" German, a language we children didn't understand. We entertained ourselves as unobtrusively as possible during the long services, ever mindful of our mothers' eyes boring into the backs of our heads from the rows of chairs behind us.

One Sunday morning, a spider made its way down the aisle, much to our squeamish enjoyment. The girl sitting next to me moved her foot slowly out into the aisle and squashed it. After the service was over, we pretended we had attended its funeral and walked reverently past the "body."

On the Sundays between the preacher's once-a-month visits, the men took turns reading German sermons from a big gray volume. One Sunday, we children must have been more unruly than usual, for my great-uncle, who had read the sermon that day, told us afterwards the story of the boy Jesus lingering in the temple. He suggested we might try to show a little of that type of respect and attention!

Marilyn Kratz,
Neuberg Congregational Church, Rural Scotland

THOSE COUNTRY SCHOOL HOUSE Bible school days were fun, being with other children, learning the Bible, and doing various drawings and posters.

I remember especially the summer I was eight. Bible school was over and it was program time. Our parents and others were coming to see our work and hear what we had learned.

I dreaded the program at that age. Being shy and lacking self-confidence, I didn't want to be in front of all the parents. However, I ended up doing all right with my part of the program.

I think what helped me get over my fear was my mother promising me a pretty new dress to wear on that special day, along with brand new white shiny patent-leather slippers. It made me feel so much better, to look nice when doing my part of the program. I do remember being happy, though, when it was over and we could enjoy the ice cream and other goodies which were waiting for us when Bible school was over for the summer. And I got over my shyness when I was older.

Joyce Knock,
Rural Leola

SINCE WE WERE ALL CLOSE IN AGE, my mother stretched herself that Sunday morning to get dinner in the oven and all seven of us ready and out the door on time. The chickens we had butchered on Saturday were in the oven, all the children were present and accounted for, and Mom felt pretty good sitting quietly in the full pew with her young family singing the hymns and looking like cherubs. Oops, too quiet, in fact. She glanced down the pew and with horror realized that her youngest, a boy, had confiscated the chicken feet and was amusing himself and everyone behind us by pulling the tendons to have the feet "walk" along the top of the pew. We're still not sure how he got those by Mom's pre-church inspection, but for a long time afterwards, he was frisked on his way out the door to church.

Carol Danielson Larson,
Sun Prairie Baptist Church, Rural Salem

IN THE 1940'S, my father, the Rev. James Driving Hawk, was in charge of an Indian community church on the Rosebud Reservation. My mother, Rose, had the responsibility of organizing the garments and shoes from the mission boxes donated by kindly women of wealthy Episcopal churches in New England.

It was exciting when the boxes came, and I helped Mom unpack them. I remember unfolding a lustrous, satin ball gown, with glittery "jewels," but an ugly brown stain on the skirt spoiled its beauty. There were fancy shoes such as high-heeled slippers with teeny straps over the toes. Then there were glossy patent leather men's shoes that went with shiny coats with long split tails, white bibs, and black bow ties. My parents laughed at the impracticality of such things on the reservation, but when Mom let me, it was fun to play "dress up."

Mission box time was also disappointing because our family never got first pick of the practical dresses, underwear, trousers, shirts, shoes, and coats. "The people need them, more than we do," Mom gently explained.

One winter I had grown so tall so fast that my winter coat was way too small. I prayed for a just-my-size coat to come in a mission box. My present coat had been so big when I got it that the sleeves had hung over my fingers, so I'd have growing room. Now it hung above my knees and my wrists stuck out like skinny sticks.

I came home from school one day to find that the boxes had arrived. Eagerly, I helped unpack them, and there was the most beautiful coat I had every seen. "Ooh," I said, as I stroked the smooth, gray, soft fur and put it on, enthralled with its sleek warmth. It was a bit long, and I could wrap it around me twice, but with all my heart I wanted that coat. Of course, I couldn't have it, but every day after school I looked to see if it was still hanging in the box room. One day it was gone, and I was heartbroken.

The next day was cold and rainy, and it was a bitter walk to school. In the cloak room, hanging on the first hook, was that fur coat.

After school, the Episcopal kids went to the guildhall for our weekly youth meeting. The rain had turned to sleet as Pauline and I waded and slipped in the gumbo. "I'm so glad I got this fur coat," she said (I thought she gloated). "It's so warm and keeps me dry. Aren't you cold?"

Miserably, I nodded. I saw out of the corner of my eye that the coat dragged on the ground; its hem was wet and splashed with mud. In the guildhall we stood near the woodstove to warm ourselves before the meeting. Soon a dank aroma filled the room as our damp coats steamed and dried.

"Phew," one of the boys said. "Pauline, your coat smells like a wet dog," and everyone laughed.

Now, I was glad not to own the coat, and Pauline, embarrassed by the "wet dog" remark, never wore it again.

Virginia Driving Hawk Sneve,
Calvary Episcopal Mission Church, Okreek

EACH YOUNG PERSON who attended our church had a rite of passage in the last week or two of the three-year confirmation course—reading his or her "I Believe" statement in front of the whole church.

This was the remnant of an old tradition, still in practice when my father was confirmed in the early 1940's, of the congregation testing confirmands about their knowledge of the Bible and Luther's Catechism. That was apparently sort of like a quiz show—"Who Wants to be a Lutheran?" rather than "Who Wants to be a Millionaire?"

But by the early 1970's, we 13-year-olds completing confirmation merely had to write two- or three-page statements of what we had learned. This was after weeks of discussion, private agony, and a meeting with the minister who, in his kindly way, suggested to the kids with the best essays (at least among the boys) that they might want to consider becoming ministers. Most of us smiled and gulped and said we'd think about it—but none of my generation of Canovans became ministers.

Since confirmation was always on Palm Sunday, we normally read our statements at a Lenten service. With hair slicked, ties (and stomach muscles) knotted, dresses just so, we waited our turns in the little wooden church on the prairie, as, more often than not, a brisk March wind blew outside. I knew from personal experience that you could hear that wind whistle through the steeple if you sat in the back row of the balcony; it added a sobering reminder of the seriousness of the Easter season, a sense that I can still recreate when I think back to that time.

Anyway, we all got through our "I Believe" statements, much to the relief of our families and, no doubt, to the disappointment of a few friends who had already lived through it and were looking forward to new reasons to tease us—and probably some of us even believed everything we said. Now we could go to communion with the grown-ups and even have that monthly hit of bad white wine that those of us who had served for communion had been wondering about for the last couple of years.

James Marten,
Immanuel Lutheran Church, Canova

THE CATHOLIC BISHOP CAME TO WOONSOCKET, my father Francis Dunn's hometown, once a year to confirm a fresh flock. Before the bishop's arrival, there was a flurry of preparation, memorization, and agonizing over which questions he might ask.

On the day of my father's confirmation, the church was filled with the families of the candidates for confirmation and with other parish members, with the young people to be questioned sitting erect in their best outfits in the front row. Each was terrified of being unable to answer a question and being humiliated.

After easing the tension a little with comparatively easy questions, the bishop cleared his throat and asked: "If your mother was dying and not expected to live through the day, what would be the most appropriate thing for you to do?"

There was a moment of nervous silence. Then one of the boys in my father's group stood up excitedly and shouted:

"Why, I'd jump on ol' Snowball and ride like the dickens for the doctor!"

Rebecca Dunn,
St. Wilfred's Catholic Church, Woonsocket

CONFIRMATION WAS ALWAYS AN IMPORTANT EVENT in the life of a Norwegian Lutheran child. It was no exception for me. I was living with my grandmother and her two bachelor sons. My grandmother was determined that I was going to be well-versed in the lessons of the church. Each Saturday morning for a year, Rev. Melling conducted catechism in the strictest of teaching environments. Occasionally he would pick me up and give me a ride. I felt safest hugging the door while enduring the silent trip to the church. Every following Friday after evening supper, Grandma would sit me down and ask me the questions over the material I was supposed to have learned during the week. I had to answer them all right before I could go to bed. One night it was midnight before I was excused!

Finally, Confirmation Sunday arrived. Grandma was in the first pew to the left of the pulpit dressed in her Sunday best, her hat perched upon her head with a pin on the side. Rev. Melling stood in front of the five confirmands to interrogate us. I ended up standing right in front of my grandmother.

One of the last questions was addressed to the first student in line and I was the last one. None of the other four ahead of me knew the answer, but I did! I was so excited that I couldn't stand still. I was moving and twitching from the time the question was asked until it was my turn. The whole congregation knew I knew the answer and so did my grandmother.

She was so proud of me as I blurted out the answer when it was finally my turn after the smartest girl in the class had missed it. Grandma reached over and tugged on my pant leg and gave me a big smile. My grandmother was very special to me, and even as a 14-year-old boy, I knew that all the hard work had been worth it to make her happy.

Jim Gederos,
Bethel Church, Claire City

I cannot find the altar boy these days
He's slipped away, hiding behind the organ pipes
Or lying under the last row of pews
Picking off the green and faded gum left
Behind by years and years of catchumens.
I cannot find the altar boy, but here's his cassock.
The cotton folds still smell like him,
They brushed against his skin so long,
But now he's gone and left behind the cloth.
The surplice's shoulders are creased by a metal hanger.
The cincture is knotted around the wire, but hanging loose.

Do you remember how he felt walking down the aisle,
The solemn crucifix heavy against his hips—How
It was for him to sit in the server's seat,
His hand reaching behind it to feel the rough stone wall—How
The chain clinked as the thurible swung up and back
And the incense flowed out in great rushes—How
The purple parament was hung, whispering on the altar—How
The paten and cruets and flagon were placed around the veiled chalice?
Do you remember the priest's hands during lavabo—How they floated—how white, how still—in the water?

    Kyrie eleison

    Christos eleison

    Kyrie eleison

    Christos eleison

        "This is My Body" (for an altar boy on his 50th birthday)
        Darla Bielfeldt, Brookings

*Eagle Nest Butte Church, Rural Wanblee, SD.
Photo courtesy of Vine Deloria, Jr.*

*All Saints Episcopal Church, Martin, SD after the July 19, 1938 tornado.
Photo courtesy of Vine Deloria, Jr.*

*Rural Martin, SD: Grace Church, before reconstruction.
Photo courtesy of Vine Deloria, Jr.*

*Grace Church after reconstruction.
Photo courtesy of Vine Deloria, Jr.*

Zion Norwegian Lutheran Church of Dumarce Township, rural Veblen, SD. Winter storm, December of 1993. Photo courtesy of Mrs. Elsie Hilleson.

Holy Trinity Church of Bendon. Moved to Kimball, SD in 1982. Photographed by Fred M. Houda. Photo courtesy of Lucille Houda.

Calvary Episcopal Church, Okreek, SD
Photographed by Rose Ross Posey. Photo courtesy of Virginia Driving Hawk Sneve.

American Baptist Publication Society, F.D. Hall—SS Missionary.
A peddler of religious books, "Mr. Johnson, Colporteur" comes through.
Photo courtesy of South Dakota State Historical Society, State Archives.

COUNTRY CONGREGATIONS

Bloomingdale Swedish Baptist Church. Jno Johnson photo, Centerville, SD. Photo courtesy of South Dakota State Historical Society, State Archives.

Annual meeting of the Sioux Falls Baptist Association, Spencer, SD. Date unknown. Photo courtesy of South Dakota State Historical Society, State Archives.

Elim Mission Church, Stockholm, SD, before the fire.
Photo courtesy of Mauriece Southwick and Phyllis Evjen.

Elim Mission Church, Stockholm, SD, after the fire.
Photo by Lemar Lundquist. Photo courtesy of Mauriece Southwick and Phyllis Evjen.

*Evangelical Free Church, Stockholm, SD, as it looked for many years.
Photo courtesy of Mauriece Southwick.*

*Evangelical Free Church, Stockholm, SD, being demolished.
Photo courtesy of Mauriece Southwick.*

Belleview Lutheran Church, Howard, SD. Photo courtesy of Duane Sander.

*Belleview Lutheran Church altar, rural Howard, SD.
Photo courtesy of Duane Sander.*

COUNTRY CONGREGATIONS

The altar of Briem Church, near Reed, Norway. Photographed by Betty Lusk. Photo courtesy of Duane Sander.

Briem Church, near Reed, Norway. Photographed by Betty Lusk. Photo courtesy of Duane Sander.

First church in Dakota. Logs hauled and church built in August, 1890, Vermillion, SD, under Rev. C.D. Martin, Presbyterian. Drawing courtesy of South Dakota State Historical Society, State Archives.

Cooks, waiters and waitresses for the German Baptist Dakota Conference, June 1909. Johannestal Baptist Church, Petersburg Township, McPherson County. Donor Mr. & Mrs. Garvin Bertsch. Photo courtesy of South Dakota State Historical Society, State Archives.

Easter Sunday program.
Photo courtesy of South Dakota State Historical Society, State Archives.

Bishop Stariha, taken on the front porch of the Old Rousseau House at the mouth of Rousseau Creek, during the Indian Congress at St. Peter's Church, July 1904.
Photo courtesy of South Dakota State Historical Society, State Archives.

Old Indian Church, northwest of Stockholm, SD. Built by the Indians of Brown Earth Settlement in 1877. Photo courtesy of South Dakota State Historical Society, State Archives.

Gladys Hawk (in wagon) with her brother Nelson Young-Hawk and her mother Elizabeth Young-Hawk, holding baby Benedict. The family walked to church, children riding in the wagon, a Christmas present from their father. Photo taken by Sam Red Horse, July 1941. Photo courtesy of Gladys Hawk.

THE LITTLE COUNTRY CHURCH that I attended as a child offered a variety of religious opportunities. The one-room church, with its gleaming white wood exterior and tall tin steeple with a cross on top, was always filled on Sunday mornings. Each family had their own pew or spot in a pew, which never changed. Our pew had held four generations of my family, who had sat on it and worn the pine seat shiny with 100 years of sitting. Sunday school was always a must for me, and I still remember my dedicated teachers, my favorite being my Uncle Ted.

Confirmation had great significance in our church. First, it required two years of study, meeting every Saturday with the minister. Also, because all the area churches were small, three were combined for Confirmation. Therefore, I studied with peers from the "Town Church" and the "North Church." That led to some competition regarding which church was the best. A wrong answer would frequently lead to snickers, especially from the North Church members.

For two years, we studied from *Luther's Small Catechism* and received our minister's additional insights. We memorized the meanings of Biblical concepts, read material assigned, and tried to become informed soon-to-be members of the church. Part of the task of the two years was overcoming the resistance to devoting every Saturday afternoon to study and our lack of enthusiasm for memorizing long paragraphs about the meaning of "things." Trying to focus on Saturday was also hard because, after a while, you got to know the attendees from the other churches, and it was fun to catch up (by whispering) about the news of the past week. An unexpected pleasure would be to get let out a bit early and walk "downtown" to window-shop or meet cousins.

Confirmation also represented a passage from childhood to adulthood. Not only would you become a church member, but you would be entering adolescence and, soon, adulthood. As Confirmation Sunday neared, I also realized that each of us needed to respond to a question that would be asked during the service. The question would be from the Catechism book. My fear was that, if I couldn't answer the questions, I would "flunk" Confirmation and have to do two more years. My panic reached high levels, until about two weeks prior to the service. Rev. Thompson, who I later realized wanted us to look intelligent, told us to "really study" the two questions he was assigning to each of us. I learned the answers perfectly and my confidence returned.

On Confirmation Sunday, I sat in the front rows with my class. In my Uncle John's wool suit, I rose, when called upon, and answered my expected questions without fear. Later my family all came to our farm home to celebrate my transition, and Mom served coffee and home-made cake. It has been 58 years since my Confirmation day, and I no longer remember my questions. But I do remember the emotion of standing tall, as I responded, feeling very dressed-up in my uncle's suit, knowing that I had really left childhood and entered another and very important stage of life.

Marvin A. Johnson,
Trinity Lutheran Church, Rural Platte

That Time of the Year

THE AREA WHERE THE OLD MEETING HOUSE once stood is now covered with water. It was located below what is now the St. Elizabeth Church. Just west of the meeting house was a log cabin where the women cooked for the festive occasion of Christmas. I remember so well the smell of fresh apples hung on strings from the ceiling, and the ladies peeling apples and rolling dough for apple pie, while the men brought in armloads of wood for the kitchen stoves. I can still hear the joking and laughing, which seemed to never end as they worked.

I also remember running away from the chickens as their heads were chopped off and they flopped around, and the smell of feathers as the ladies dunked them in tubs of hot water to make it easier to pluck their feathers. Everyone pitched in to help with whatever was needed. We kids just had fun watching and finding ways to keep ourselves occupied.

When I went outside in the dark of night, I could smell fresh hay and hear the horses as they crunched on the hay and the occasional whinny of a colt when it strayed from its mother. I remember I always went to the outhouse with my mom so we could watch the door for each other. An old pump was used to water the horses. Sometimes it was late at night before we started for home.

We children could hardly contain ourselves as we watched the adults getting ready for the big day. I remember that an uncle, Zidol Red Horse, Big Sis Nora's dad, brought the pine tree in his sleigh, and it seemed to be the biggest Christmas tree in the world. The men folk then brought in their gas lamps and made sure they were in working order. I can still see them as they pumped the lamps and put fresh mantels in the globes. The potbelly stove stood in the middle of the meeting room with a big coffee pot on top of it, and the aroma of fresh coffee permeated the room. Someone played the pump organ and we sang hymns in Lakota. The walls of the old meeting house seemed to sway with the swell of the songs. Those oldtimers could really sing.

Gladys Hawk,
St. Elizabeth Episcopal Church, Wakpala

"Now, don't go and throw peanuts this year, OK?" Mom asked. "Sure, Mom," I agreed. What? No peanuts? Weren't we going to get our usual bag of peanuts after the Sunday school program? And besides, I wasn't the one throwing them anyway. Usually, I was one of the targets and had learned to move quickly up and down the basement steps and sometimes out the side door to avoid being thwapped on the head with an empty peanut shell.

I was the third generation of a Danish family which had been attending this church since emigrating early in the century. This Christmas, our Sunday School program was held on the Sunday night before Christmas in order to allow for one more rehearsal after church that day. All 31 Sunday school students were re-enacting the "Greatest Story Ever Told" while dressed in plaid bathrobes, blue shawls, and white dish towels draped over their heads and held in place with very long shoestrings. We had seen pictures of an elaborate nativity scene re-enacted in LIFE magazine, but because we were a farming community, no one even suggested bringing in a sheep or two from Brown's pasture for authenticity. That picture in LIFE was part of our daily reality, and no one in the congregation had trouble imagining the shuffling of cattle's hooves, the satisfied grunts of feeding piglets and, of course, the smell. In fact, I had often wondered about God's choice of birthplace for His Only Son, but I decided it was one more thing that I would understand when I grew up.

Our choir (which was actually the entire Sunday School forced into a semblance of three orderly rows) made a joyful noise with the old carols: "O Little Town of Bethlehem," "Hark! The Herald Angels Sing," and especially "Joy to the World." No fancy choral arrangements for us; however, the little organ had a special setting for tinkling bells, and Darlene Andersen saved this feature for use only at Christmas. Those who understood a bit about harmony, usually those of us who were taking piano lessons from Eva Andersen in Hetland, ventured to sing a bit of alto or tenor. Our parents and teachers joined us in singing the final "Joy to the

World." Garrison Keillor is right about the gusto Lutherans can create while singing beloved hymns! However, this year Darlene asked me to sing a solo: Verse Three of "O Come, O Come Immanuel," (page 71 in the Junior Hymnal) Wow, me, a solo? My very practical brothers quickly erased this thought of stardom by telling me that's what I got for singing so loud. When Verse Three came along, I sang it while still muffled within Row Two. No one told me to step out front—a good Lutheran doesn't draw attention to herself—and no one moved aside for me, either—no one should be putting on airs, you know.

After the program, we gathered in the church basement to eat at long wooden tables loaded with hand-decorated Christmas cookies, homemade candy, lefse (yes, there were a few renegade Norwegians in the flock), and green or red Jell-O, and to drink from large blue enamel pots of boiled coffee in which the coffee grounds had been mixed with an egg before cooking. Before we could open any presents, we all joined hands and danced around the Christmas tree—an old Danish custom that was still being practiced cheerfully in Badger. Dad remembers that we sang "Nu Har Vi Jul Agin" ("Now We Have Christmas Again") which was always sung in Danish, but the one I remember is "Little Red Caboose, chug, chug, chug..." Heaven only knew if that was an authentic Christmas song or not! Sunday school teachers were expected to give presents to each of their students, and we were expected to reciprocate, so that ensured that the Christmas tree was almost floating above a sea of presents. My teacher that year was my Aunt Ruthie, whose husband, Uncle Gordon, was a tolerably good carpenter. Expecting to receive the usual ball-point pen with a tiny picture of Jesus on it, I was thrilled to unwrap a piece of green painted wood with four holes precisely drilled across the top and four red candles—my own advent wreath! I'm afraid I gave Aunt Ruthie one of the many available forms of "Here's My Heart" fragrance purchased from the neighborhood Avon lady.

But now it was time for our final gift! Each of us "kidlets" (Grandma's way of softening "kids") received a brown paper bag of treats: hard striped candy, oddly shaped filled candy, a large Red Delicious apple, and, of course, unshelled peanuts. Let the party begin! Why those older boys (cousins Randy and Arthur especially) thought it was the height of entertainment to hit us younger kids with peanut shells, I'll never know, but I do know the mess we made in the narthex and basement stairwell of Bethany Lutheran that frosty Christmas and every year during the time-honored Christmas peanut fight.

Our Christmas Eve service at Bethany Lutheran was much more civilized, however, and perhaps that's why we never had our Sunday school program on Christmas Eve—we understood our limits! The service began that Christmas Eve at 4:30 p.m. while there was still light in the sky. Candles burned in homemade decorated wooden holders in the windowsills, and as we sang "Silent Night," each of us received the "Light of the World" from the person seated next to us. One of the ushers turned off the glaring electric lights, leaving the small church lit only with the soft glow from each small candle. What a deeply moving moment—or it was until my two brothers decided to play "sword fight" with their lighted candles and almost began the great Badger conflagration! Pastor Melby warned us: "Don't dip the lighted candle!" But his warning was to no avail, as red taffeta jumpers and slightly wrinkled suit pants went home with spots of candle wax on them.

The most wonderful moment of Christmas Eve was when we opened the church doors after the service and found that huge fluffy flakes of snow were falling, turning the evening into a fairytale setting that would inspire even the most stubborn Danish curmudgeon. Then the entire Jensen family gathered at Grandma's and Grandpa's house for our Christmas feast, which included Danish Kringle, apple-walnut dressing, and Grandma's red cabbage...but that's another story!

Our church closed its doors in 1965 and merged with First English Lutheran Church just down the street; together we became Badger Lutheran Church. The councils decided to use the First English facility, as it was larger and had indoor plumbing. A few years later, the building which had been our church was sold to Kingsbury County, and now its front doors open to house a road grader within those hallowed walls.

> Jane Pierce,
> Bethany Lutheran Church, Badger

OUR DIMINUTIVE COUNTRY CHURCH is nestled between two stately evergreens with its steeple rising above both of them, reaching to the heavens. The church, with its arched windows and front steps that encourage me to enter, seems to have stepped out of a Christmas card depicting days gone by. I have been blessed to have been an active part of my church's Christmas setting since birth. Receiving baptismal water from the font that my grandmother's brother built with hand tools, and hearing God's word read from the lectern my husband designed and built in loving memory of my father, ties me ever closer to our church.

> Joyce Poppen,
> St. John's Lutheran Church, Dempster

COUNTRY CONGREGATIONS

THE LITTLE WHITE CHURCH stood next to the road on Three Mile Creek. St. Sophie's, a small church by today's reckoning, would seat maybe 50 worshipers. A pump organ and an ornate wood altar graced the front of the church. A wood-burning stove stood to the left of the communion rail. A statue to the right kept watch as parishioners went to the confessional.

The Meeting Hall at Sophie's seemed large to us. A pot-bellied stove stood at one end and a cook stove at the other end. Christmas Day was special in the Hall—a mystical event for children. For me, 1948 was especially memorable.

I always looked forward to the preparation—cooking, baking, gift-wrapping. Everything was secretive. I remember Mom and Grandma would "talk Lakota" when the planning didn't include me!

On Christmas Eve, we would gather at Grandma's and Grandpa's place. Grandma would serve a delicious supper, and after the dishes were cleared, we would exchange gifts. Grandpa would take out his violin and we would sing Christmas carols until it was time to head for Midnight Mass at Our Lady of Sorrows in Kyle.

Christmas Day was reserved for family day at St. Sophie's on Three Mile, but in 1948, Old Man Winter seemed to have other ideas. For several days, the snows came. There would be no Midnight Mass this year. Maybe there would not even be Christmas Day at the Meeting Hall!

But on Christmas Day we awakened to beautiful sunshine. We had no bobsled, so my uncle improvised. The tractor was hooked to his hayrack for our Christmas taxi! With presents, cakes, pies and pots of soup and my sisters tied behind the rack on sleds, our family made it through the deep snow for the two-mile journey to the church. Other families had come on horseback, by horse-drawn wagons, or on foot.

Mass that morning was special, as was the breakfast. The men popped the corn on the pot-bellied stove. The women made taffy. Someone shouted: "All those who want to help make popcorn balls— go wash your hands!" If our hands passed inspection, they were greased with lard and we could join in the fun of making the popcorn balls.

We played in the new snow all afternoon. Then, from the meeting hall, came the call "Supper!" The excitement built. Santa was coming soon! When it was dark, we heard the dancing of hooves on the meeting hall roof!

There were presents for all. Christmas Day had come in spite of the deep snow. Our uncle had seen to that. His "Hay-rack Christmas Taxi" made 1948 one of my fondest family memories.

Violet Van Deest,
Saint Sophie's Church, Rural Kyle

CHRISTMAS WAS ANYTHING BUT MERRY for our family one year. That Christmas Eve, as we were getting ready to go to church for the Sunday school's Christmas program, our family dog Sandy was killed by a passing car. My younger sisters, the twins Jeannette and Joanne, who were about eight, and Alma, who was about ten, were especially upset. Sandy, of a breed sometimes referred to as "the neighborhood's best," was a lovable mutt who had been a member of our family for a long time. To add to our preparation complications, the electricity went out, and the house was as dark as our moods as we struggled to get ready.

At the church, my little sisters' red eyes were evidence of the flow of tears before the program, as they bravely struggled to perform their parts. Altogether, however, the timing of the event was probably a good thing, as it and the distribution of sacks of candy which followed it provided at least temporary comfort for my sorrowful little sisters.

Luella DeJong,
Trinity Lutheran Church, Tea

GRANT CENTER CHRISTMAS. I remember the Christmas tree that sat on the left side of the pulpit and reached the ceiling. It was decorated with tinsel, strings of cranberries and popcorn, and real candles. After the Christmas Eve service and children's program, Santa Claus came. He passed out gifts to the littlest children. I remember getting a boy doll. Each of the children got a LARGE bag of nuts and candy. The men of the church put them together, and each bag cost them about twenty-five cents.

> *Arvel Trapp,*
> *Grant Center Evangelical United, Brethren Church*

THE LUTHER LEAGUE was in charge of decorating our church for Christmas. For several years, my father, who managed the Co-op Lumber Yard in Canova, volunteered his time and the lumberyard truck to fetch a giant tree from a farm near Baltic. Once it was delivered, the first job of the decorating crew was to pull, push, and otherwise convince the tree to squeeze through the double doors in the back of the church. Without adult supervision, we Luther Leaguers also dangled from big wooden extension ladders to hang garlands and lights from the arch above the altar. Once, after fetching a box of decorations from the old parsonage a hundred yards from the church, I was walking back toward the church when I heard a tremendous, discordant tone followed by the higher sound of breaking glass. I rushed back to the church, where I found that in moving the big upright piano out of the way, some of my young colleagues had pushed it over; its falling had caused a light in the downstairs hallway to crash to the floor. Remember, there was no adult supervision!

> *James Marten,*
> *Immanuel Lutheran Church, Canova*

"Julotta" at Highlanda Lutheran Church in rural Langford means having Christmas morning service at 6 a.m. The first members brought their Swedish customs from the "old country." In Sweden, it was the custom of families to rise early and light candles in their home windows "to light the Christ child on His way." Swedish legend says that the Christ child was born just before dawn. Church services are held with many candles lit around the altar and windows.

Over the years, the many pastors of our church have adopted the Julotta tradition. Every year the congregation, along with visitors, joins in singing the first verse of the hymn "When Christmas Morn is Dawning" in Swedish: "Nar juldagsmorgan glimmar." Then we exclaim together: "God Jul!"

Highland Lutheran Church Senior Members, Rural Langford

We always attended the early morning Julotta service, unless there was a blizzard. I remember getting up as an older child on Christmas morning at 4:30 a.m. Dad would go out and feed and harness the team of horses, while Mother would see to it that we children got dressed warmly in long-legged underwear, over-the-knee home-knit wool stockings, caps and scarves, and home-knit wool mittens. Then we warmed blankets and heated rocks to keep our feet warm, and all got into a double wagon box, which was set on sled runners, and were off on a seven-mile ride to the church. There were sleigh bells on the horses. The church lights were such a welcome sight. Going home was not so comfortable at times because the blankets and rocks would be cold, but the morning star in the east would be so bright and guide us. It was so good to get home to a house warmed by a hard coal heater.

Highland Lutheran Church Senior Members, Rural Langford

I LIVED NEAR THE CHURCH, so at age 15, I was the janitor. I would miss a night's sleep on Christmas Eve, because after having Christmas Eve activities at home, I had to keep the furnace going at the church so that it was warm at 6 a.m. If you got to church early, you might get your horse in the church barn. After services, the Swedes hurried home. According to legend, the first one home would get the best crop! After returning home from Julotta, families often enjoyed foods such as ost kaka, sot ost and doppa. (Doppa means "dipping of bread in the pot.")

Highland Lutheran Church Senior Members, Rural Langford

THE JULOTTA SERVICE THAT I RECALL THE MOST was when I was seven years old. Arrangements had been made for me to stay home with my brother and my grandmother, but I awoke early and begged to go along and my parents relented. The service began at 5 a.m. We lived seven miles from the church. When we arrived, only seats toward the front were available. There was a grate in the center of the church for heat from the coal furnace. Two services were held, one in Swedish, and the other in English, each lasting a full hour. The beautifully decorated candle-lit church failed to keep me awake, and I dozed on my mother's shoulder, regretting having left my warm bed.

Pearl Lundquist,
Tabor Evangelical Lutheran Church, Strandburg

COUNTRY CONGREGATIONS

SNOW LAY IN DEEP FOLDS around the little Spirit Lake Presbyterian Church. Stars twinkled in the sky, although the moon was not in sight this Christmas Eve in 1918. Because the roads and the churchyard were deeply covered in snow, bobsleds pulled by teams brought the families with excited children to the Christmas program. Families swathed in mufflers and coats piled out of the sleds by the church door and fathers drove the teams up to the hitching posts that stretched behind the church.

I was an excited young girl dressed in my best with my hair carefully fixed with bows. I stood in the back of the church and caught my breath. The front of the church was decorated and a white paper bell was hung. The center of attention was a tall evergreen tree. Red and white paper chains encircled the branches as well as strings of popcorn and cranberries. What was very special was that real candles were on the branches. The holders had little metal clips and in each holder was a tall candle.

In those days we were all used to real flames. Our kerosene lamps were flames. In the stoves in our homes, fires burned. Still, candles on a tree were very special. We all knew that a pail of water was underneath the front bench, near the tree. We also knew that Uncle Mun would watch the tree carefully. He was a tall man and in charge of the candles. He had a candlesnuffer with a good handle in his hands. He examined the candles on the tree one last time before lighting them. He would light them just at the beginning of the service. Then he stood there by the tree watching the program and his candles. The last thing on the program was "Silent Night." As the last "Sleep in Heavenly Peace" was completed, a child would usually call out: "I think one's going to burn there!" It never did, for as the song closed, the snuffer covered each candle until the lights were out for another year at the Spirit Lake Church. Now those candles shine only in memory.

Ann Poppen Cramer's story told by Marian Cramer,
Spirit Lake Presbyterian Church

WHEN I WAS A YOUNG LADY, I had a bad experience. As I lit the real candles on our home Christmas tree, I started at the lower branches and worked up to the top, leaning close. Then my dress caught on fire! I screamed, and Mom and Dad came running. I had batted the flames with my hands and put out the fire.

Then we went to evening services at church where there was a large Christmas tree, bedecked with clip-on candleholders with real candles. I shrank back at the sight! Then somebody lit the candles and I looked frantically around for a quick escape route! Nothing happened, however, thank God. Still, I never trusted real candle flame around a real evergreen Christmas tree again.

These electric tree lights are oh so much more delightful!

Myra D. Kalb,
West Wall Lake Lutheran Church

THE ANNUAL SUNDAY SCHOOL CHRISTMAS PROGRAM was an important event. The girls looked forward to the time when they could be chosen to play the part of Mary. I don't know if the boys felt that way about being chosen to play the role of Joseph.

One Christmas in the mid 1940's, our Sunday School Superintendent, Marie Vig, had several of us girls dressed in long white flowing cheesecloth gowns and wearing crowns of white candles. We sang, "Will There Be Any Stars in Our Crown?" We continued singing as we slowly walked down the aisle. It was so quiet and the people were wiping tears from their eyes.

At the end of the program, the Sunday school students joined hands and walked around the altar, singing "Here We Go Around The Christmas Tree." The decorated tree with the small white candles stood inside the altar ring.

The traditional bags of peanuts, hard Christmas candy and apples, with one piece of soft candy per sack, were given out to everyone. For some of us, that one piece of chocolate candy was eaten immediately, while for others it was taken home and nibbled on for a few days, to savor the sweetness.

Norma Johnson,
Bethel Lutheran Church, Rural Claire City

WHEN I WAS IN HIGH SCHOOL, the Luther League was given responsibility for conducting Christmas candlelight services and Easter Sunrise services. We felt ourselves to be quite creative when we used modern (at least by 1970's small-town standards) narrative techniques to tell these ageless stories: one year, the nativity story was told as a "You Are There" show, with the entire front of the church substituting for Bethlehem. The host (me) interviewed shepherds on the altar steps, the innkeeper at the door of the storage closet behind the organ, and Mary and Joseph themselves in front of the white and gilt altar which had been imported generations before from England. On another occasion, the phenomena of the resurrection was analyzed by a battery of guests on a talk show hosted—again—by me. The adults kindly complimented us on our daring interpretation of the old stories, but it was never clear to me if they really appreciated the application of modern formats to ancient traditions.

James Marten,
Immanuel Lutheran Church, Canova

ST. PAUL LUTHERAN HAS MANY WOMEN WHO ANSWER, "Sure, if you need me." And answer it the same pleasant way year after year. One program stands out in my mind.

Pat had been scheduled for the Christmas program, but her mother passed away December 5. The following year she and her teenage son gave "Let There Be Peace On Earth and Let It Begin With Me."

Our chairs were grouped in a loose circle with a large rectangle of green poster board on the floor. Pat began with an explanation, scripture and prayer, and Christmas music. Her son Douglas handed each of us a jigsaw puzzle piece approximately 4 x 4 inches. Each piece had been cut from a map and on each was a sparkly letter of the alphabet. On the back of each piece was a typed reading.

This one said, "I received the letter N. I pray for neighbors. Thank you for neighbors. Bless our neighbors close to us in our daily lives and also our neighbors in the broader sense of the world." Below that was this:

"Mark 12:33: And to love him with all the heart and with all the understanding, and with all the soul, and with all the strength, and to love his neighbor as himself, is more than all the whole burnt offerings and sacrifices."

After each puzzle piece was read, it was set in approximately the correct map place.

It didn't take long for us to see what we had! It was a world map. As the rectangle of the world took shape on the dark green background, the large, gold glitter letters stood out clearly: "Let There Be Peace On Earth And Let It Begin With Me."

After the program closed, the puzzle was taken apart and the pieces were put by the exit doors. Each person was encouraged to take home a piece, to use throughout the year. It was a reminder to each of us "to really let peace begin with me."

Doris Hanson,
St. Paul Lutheran, Rural Elk Point

I HAVE MANY FOND MEMORIES of my childhood, but one New Year's gathering stands out from the rest. We were all up very early; it was a cold winter day, December 31, 1923. There were so many things to pack for our trip by wagon to the New Year's gathering at the Red Hall in Parmelee, eight miles from our home. My father had gone after the team of horses. Today we would be traveling in our farm wagon with the top box on it. I was so excited that I completely forgot about what a cold trip it would be for all of us.

Then we were ready to load the wagon. My father had put hay in the bottom of it to help us keep warm. He then loaded the mattresses, heavy quilts, trunks, a tent, cooking utensils, wood and all other necessary items for a two-day stay.

The eight-mile trip seemed to take forever. At one point, my father got out of the wagon and walked alongside of the horses to keep warm. His overboots were wrapped with burlap bags to help insulate them.

Finally, we arrived in Parmelee. There were so many camps already. I was so excited to get to the hall, but the ice and snow on the ground where we were going to make camp needed to be cleared. Hay was then placed on the ground and the tent was pitched. Soon, we had the tent up and our wagon unloaded. The camp stove filled our tent with warmth. There was lots of action, with people chopping wood, cleaning snow, scraping ice, and putting up their tents. Then, hand games and other games were played. Later, we all stopped and offered prayers of thanks to the Creator for the year that was past.

I felt I couldn't wait any longer to get to the hall. I could see people going in and out of the hall and the sounds of drums filled the cold air, inviting us to come and enjoy the festivities.

As we neared the hall, the Eyapaha, the crier, spoke to the people and their children about what was expected of them during this gathering. He said: "My relatives, I'm going to talk to you. Take care of your children. Be observant. Listen." Inside, the women were bustling around cooking and baking, and so many good smells filled the hall. Many activities took place as the evening went on, including our traditional dancing. I ate so much and joined in on the games and dancing.

Then the festivities came to a halt. We were told it was almost midnight. A prayer was said by all of the Episcopalians, Catholics, etc., and then the masquerade dancers came in, the women on the one side and the men on the other, to bring in the new year and throw out the old. One masquerader was dressed up as an old man, "The Old Year." Some men masqueraded as women, and had to continue to dance that way, even after the masks came off. I remember that one nice-looking Lakota woman always carried a doll, and when I was little I thought it was real.

Then the crier announced that it was almost time, and everyone stopped and an elder prayed. Then a man dressed as "The New Year," with the number of the year on his back, entered and pushed "The Old Year" out the door. The New Year Man always carried something to symbolize what might happen in the year ahead; for example, corn, if the crops were to be good, or a beer bottle if it was feared that there would be substance abuse. I don't remember what was carried that year. Because the gathering would last until the wee hours of the morning, beds were nearby for children. In those days, you didn't hear the crying from children like you do now. I stayed up and enjoyed myself as long as I could because I didn't want the night to end, but finally I was put in my makeshift bed to sleep. Later, my mother gently shook me and told me it was time to return to our tent. When we came out of the hall it was near morning, and we could see frost on the tents.

When I awoke, it was light and snow was falling. It was New Year's Day, 1924. We returned to the Red Hall at noon for a meal and another day of dancing and games. The festivities went on again that day and into the night. I was so tired and so full of good things to eat. Everyone retired earlier that night, because many had long trips home.

The next day it was time to return home. Goodbyes were exchanged and preparations were made. I had so much fun and visited with so many friends and relatives that I wished it would go on forever.

We returned to our cold home weary and exhausted, but I could hardly wait for New Year's, 1925.

Ollie Napesni,
St. Francis, Parmalee

EASTER MORNING DAWNED as fresh as dew-covered daffodils and sprouting seeds. When I was four, Easter seemed as new as the pink, yellow, blue, and green eggs that suddenly colored previously empty places around our farmhouse and yard. After gathering eggs, sweets and a yellow stuffed rabbit, my Easter basket was filled, and I scrambled indoors to prepare for Sunday school and church.

When I entered the kitchen, my eyes alighted, for the most beautiful dress I had ever seen hung against the wall. Its white satin, sprinkled with miniature blue flowers, shimmered against the wallpaper, and fragile lace trim finished the collar and sleeves. But what fascinated me the most was my first "blue ribbon"—a silk sash the shade of the sky, tied elegantly at the waist into a bow. Breath held, I drew nearer, only to discover white lace stockings, white patent-leather shoes, and white gloves fit for a four-year-old. As Mother helped me step delicately into the clothes, she explained that each little girl should have a special Easter dress, and I felt I had the finest.

Once dressed I waited anxiously for my ride to Sunday school. Each week, my dad's cousin Daryle and his children picked me up on their way to church. I always considered this a treat, because I got to see my cousins, Amy and Becky. When I climbed into their station wagon to greet them that Easter morning, they were wearing special Easter dresses, too. I admired their silken blond hair and equally pretty dresses, and we smiled at each other in delight while we drove the three graveled miles to church.

When we arrived, Daryle carefully lined us up for a photograph in front of the church near a white sign that read, "St. John's Evangelical Lutheran Church, Dempster, SD." As Amy, Becky, and I stood closely together, I felt so happy to be in church with my two dear friends. The camera shutter clicked, capturing three innocent girls, all smiling shyly, ready to run inside and rejoice. Today, as I hold that picture in my hand, I smile still, remembering what special times those were, and how sweet it is to see girls in their Easter dresses.

Naomi Stapleton,
St John's Evangelical Lutheran Church, Dempster

"UP, FROM THE GRAVE HE AROSE" echoed, often off key, throughout the canyon in which our little group of 35 sang during a recent Easter sunrise service there. The large crowd for this busy lambing and calving time of year had found grassy spots between cow pies for their blankets. Many had already ridden horseback for a couple of hours checking calves or had been lambing sheep, and a few of those were taking this short time to catch a few winks of sleep. The emerging sun was creating a glow on the three old wooden crosses on the west bank of the canyon as the fill-in pastor read the Easter story. The dirt cliff beneath the crosses was reminiscent of an empty tomb.

Easter sunrise services in Cedar Canyon, at our Bible Camp campground in a neighbor's pasture, will always be with me. I still attend these country services whenever I get home that time of year, although I didn't often get to do that when I was young because we were usually lambing so many sheep. For some people, Easter is the only time besides Christmas or a baby baptism when they attend church. For my family, Easter was often one of the few times when we could not attend.

Instead, on those no-service Easter Sundays, we would rise early, hunt the candy eggs which the Easter bunny had hidden outdoors, and enjoy hard-boiled eggs for breakfast, complemented by Mother's homemade caramel rolls, and then either ride horseback to check cows or suckle poor-doing lambs in the lambing shed. At noon, Mother would give us a good Easter dinner of ham, mashed potatoes, and lemon pie.

The rest of the year, my family attended Sunday school, church, and vacation Bible school in a small country church a couple of miles east of Cedar Canyon on a hill between Mud Butte and Maurine. The few people who attend this church travel as far as 30 miles, not because of its fancy stained glass windows, but because of its Bible-based message. Although I now live near Belle Fourche, I continue to refer to Mud Butte and Prairie Home Church when I talk about "home."

Since we seven kids have left home, my parents have sold the big bunch of sheep. That means that we now usually have time to go to Easter sunrise services back home. We also have an Easter potluck breakfast after the service and visit with our neighbors. This is not a fancy Easter sunrise service, but at our service, the meadowlarks perched on the old wooden crosses on the canyon bank can compete with any big city church organ.

Sally M. Crouser,
Prairie Home Church, Rural Mud Butte

For the Good of the Cause

I WAS OUR CHURCH JANITOR IN THE THIRTIES, beginning when I was 13. It was a lot of hard work.

In the summer, there was lawn mowing. I had to push 12-inch "reel" mowers. If a stick or stone put a nick in the reel or got it out of alignment, the mower would not cut evenly and it had to be realigned. The blades had to be sharpened with a file before every cutting.

In the winter, there was the firing of the furnace and snow shoveling. The colder it was, the earlier the furnace had to be started. The church building was not insulated, the windows were not weather-stripped, and the ceiling was high, so it got as cold inside as out. It took many hours to get everything to an acceptable temperature—especially the benches. The furnace was in the basement, with the heat coming out of the floor toward the back of the church. The coal was "soft," dirty and dusty. Sometimes the delivery man would wet it down, which helped with the dust, but made a mess in the coal bin and the basement.

Every Wednesday afternoon was German prayer service for the elderly members and Wednesday evening was English prayer service for all of the others. I would go before school, fire the furnace, stop at noon to see if it was warm enough, leave the church unlocked for the afternoon service, and go back after school and put in a little more coal to keep the building warm for the evening service. Then I would go back again at about 9 p.m. to lock the door.

I also had to ring the church bell a half-hour before each service, morning and evening, and it had to be "tolled" for a funeral, beginning when the funeral procession came into view, and continuing until the body was removed from the hearse. After the service, the bell had to be tolled again from the time the body was placed back in the hearse until the funeral procession was again out of sight.

I also had to usher at every service, and be sure to provide a glass of water on the pulpit for the minister. I often thought about giving him a "spiked" drink, but never had the nerve.

Once a year, the Ladies' Aid put on a chicken supper in the basement. Then I had to put up tables, get chairs lined up, and provide coal in buckets beside the cook stoves.

Also, every November, there were two weeks of revival meetings, with church every night and prayer meetings every afternoon. This required quite a bit of extra cleaning and furnace firing. I was expected to be at all services "to take care of things," and at times I began to think I was "over-churched."

In any event, this job made me appreciate the better things that were to come, and better working conditions, and better pay.

Kermit Liebing,
Evangelical Church, Milbank

OUR CONGREGATION CONSISTED OF HARD-WORKING farm families. Some had a little less than others, but no one really knew the difference. The church raised money through the revenue from crops produced on an acreage donated by one of the families. Others would provide equipment, and still others would provide labor. All felt equally important to the giving ministry of the church.

That experience taught me that "tithe" is measured not only in money, but in time and labor and equipment, and that everyone is important in God's eyes and all have a part to play.

Rep. Orv Smidt,
Sterling Methodist Church, Rural Brookings

IN THE WINTER, THE YOUTH FELLOWSHIP would sponsor fox and rabbit hunts. Groups of men would gather at the church and hunt the sections—starting on the outside and working their way to the middle. We'd hear "Fox going north!" and the hunters on that side would get ready to shoot. The skins were valuable then and they were sold to raise money for the church. The ladies would have hot soup waiting for us in the church basement when we got back.

Duane Bohn,
Twin Brooks Evangelical Church

ONE FALL THE WEATHER WAS SUCH that the corn was falling off the stalks. A bachelor farmer who lived in a one-room house near Peever donated to the church the corn in one of his fields that was left after he'd harvested. The entire congregation went to the corn field on a Sunday afternoon and we picked the fallen ears and piled them in wagons. The money from the corn supplemented our church budget. Everyone from little kids to adults worked the field together on that cool, crisp autumn day.

Gail Ramynke,
Peever Lutheran Church

OUR CHURCH WOMEN HAVE ALWAYS QUILTED. In the early days, women walked, rode horses, and drove buggies to each others' houses to quilt. The Busy Bees, an early quilting group, made money to fund the altar which still graces our church.

All-day quiltings happen now in January, February, March, and August. Members gather materials wherever we can—from second-hand stores and bargain sales, and by cleaning out our own closets. Co-chairmen, and sometimes helpful husbands, set up the quilt frames made by the men in the congregation, haul out the supplies on two rolling carts built for that purpose, start the coffee, keep count of our accumulating finished quilts, and pack them for delivery.

We have sack lunches and short business meetings at noon, and morning and afternoon coffee breaks. We work hard, talk fast, and snack often. Jokes, laughter, sharing of opinions, and neighborhood news keep minds busy as hands cut, sew, press, tie, pin, and hem through the day. If the talk stills, quiet music from the public radio station can be heard in the background, sometimes interrupted by gentle jibes about the need for "coffee time." By the afternoon coffee break, most of us are tired enough to begin picking up and packing away until the next time, when the tradition will continue.

Doris Hanson,
St. Paul Lutheran Church, Rural Elk Point

Uninvited Guests

WE HAD SOME DOINGS AT CHURCH and a mouse came running right across the piano keys. My sister Eileen was the pianist. Us girls were sitting in the front row and we were wondering what she was going to do about that mouse—if she was gonna scream or what. But she kept right on a-playing, and it ran down and then into the choir someplace. You don't forget stuff like that.

> *Shirley Hansen,*
> *Grant Center Evangelical United Brethren Church,*
> *Rural Milbank*

OFTEN, WHEN THE WEATHER WAS PLEASANT, my husband took our dog along when he went to conduct church services at Fairburn. The dog usually waited patiently outside until the service was over, except for one Sunday when she ran into the church and went to the piano and stayed there for the entire service. When the service was over, some of the men moved the piano and the dog caught the mouse which had been hiding there.

Darlene Finney,
Fairburn Methodist Church

I WAS AN USHER, and we always wore white shirts and coats and ties, no matter how hot it was. In the summer, we'd open the windows for fresh air, and not all of the windows had screens on them. I remember one time a pigeon came in through the window and sat on the choir loft railing.

Duane Bohn,
Twin Brooks Evangelical, United Brethren Church

I WAS ONLY TEN YEARS OLD. Our pastor's sermon echoed in the background like a broadcast on the radio with the dial turned low. Suddenly my attention centered on the box elder bug crawling on the back of Robert Temple's suit coat collar, just about to go off the creased edge onto his neck. I watched anxiously for minutes the black-winged red-bodied creature with two dark feelers and three delicate matching legs on either side of his almond-shaped body.

It never stopped moving, going back and forth over Robert's collar, onto his shoulder, down his sleeve and back to his collar. It seemed lost, and frantically looking for its home or a place to rest.

At last it crawled onto Robert's neck. Robert was half asleep, so the bug startled him, and he jumped up, and swiped at his neck, trying to remove whatever was tickling him. I sat behind him smirking and desperately trying to hold my laughter in. We were not allowed to even fidget in church, let alone laugh, or we'd be in big trouble when we got home. All caught up in my anticipation of the box elder bug's reaching Robert's neck, I hadn't noticed my father's watchful eye on me. Dad's stern eye contact wiped the smirk off my face immediately.

I never really understood what God's intention was for the box elder bug. I only knew that in the autumn as the wind blew more from the north, the box elders suddenly appeared. The crack lines of the painted concrete foundation would appear to be in movement from all the red and black soldiers marching in formation. As a child, I wondered where they had been all summer, and where they had gone when they had disappeared. In any event, I suppose it's good that they only attend church seasonally.

Joyce Poppen,
St. John's Lutheran Church, Dempster

ONE HOT SUMMER SUNDAY on the Rosebud reservation, we were celebrating the Holy Eucharist in the front room of a home, with about a dozen people sitting on chairs and against the walls. During a quiet moment in the service, a young deer walked in the front door, looked around, and then calmly walked through the front room and kitchen and exited out the back door. No one in the congregation commented or seemed surprised.

I continued on with the service, but that moment made a deep impression on me and has remained in my memory. I don't know what it meant to the others present, but for me, it was as if, just for a moment, God's peaceable kingdom had arrived, and in that instant, there was a glimpse of the day when the lion and the lamb, the hunter and the hunted, will lie down together in peace.

Father Fred Jessett,
St. Andrew's Episcopal Church, Spring Creek

Outside Interests

Picturesque rural churches, their spires spiking the sky, often had behind them...outhouses, kept in pristine condition by the annual scrubbings and paintings of their fastidious members. The outhouse was just as important as the pulpit or the organ. In fact, for many years after its congregation disbanded, the outhouse of the Powell Presbyterian Church south of Ipswich offered a haven for many a traveler along that desolate stretch of Highway 45.

The outhouse of my childhood church had, for whatever reason, the unique feature of a lock on the outside of the door as well as one on the inside, and these were sturdy hook-and-eye gadgets that held as fast as the chains of Hell.

One Sunday morning while we awaited the arrival of our pastor from our sister congregation at Wecota, I slipped out to the outhouse. But unbeknownst to me, the two youngest Perry boys had slipped out behind me, and as I shot the hook in place on the inside, they were doing the same on the outside.

Amazingly, as soon as I realized my predicament, I didn't panic. "Pretty soon," I told myself, "my folks will come looking for me." But then I noticed, in the corner above the door, spiders—not cute, clumsy daddy-longlegs—but huge, fat specimens, the kind that inhabit your nightmares.

And then the screaming began. I was known far and wide for my scream, and that Sunday morning I gave it my all. Surprisingly, I didn't shatter the stained glass windows in the church.

Now, when a pastor served two congregations, time was of the essence. Our pastor would time his departure from Wecota to the second and then tear down the gravel road, often at an outrageous speed. He would leap from his car, bound up the church steps, and stride down the aisle just as the prelude was ending.

On this particular morning as he got out of his car, he was greeted by the most gosh-awful shrieking imaginable. Without missing a beat and with robes flying, he detoured around to the outhouse, flipped the hook, and, not even looking back to see the source of the caterwauling, continued into the church.

Oh, the conflicting emotions I felt—relief at being freed, embarrassment that it was the pastor who had freed me, and rage at those Perry boys!

I'm happy to say that I suffered no adverse affects from my experience—no claustrophobia, no inordinate fear of spiders—and to this day I count the two young men involved among my closest friends. Now, had it been a snake in that outhouse instead of spiders—that would have been a different story!

Maxine Hansen Swanson,
Concordia Lutheran Church, Cresbard

OUR LITTLE COUNTRY CHURCH was a very strict denomination, not believing in such vices as smoking or drinking.

There was a pretty girl in this church and a young man from town started coming out to church to see her.

Well, the preacher's little son Bobby, about five or six at the time, saw something interesting in the young man's car as he walked by it and happened to peek in the window.

On the seat lay a pack of cigarettes and some matches. This was too much of a temptation for Bobby. He quickly opened the door and grabbed that pack of interesting things along with the matches. Then he hurried off to show his three little buddies his prize. Where would they go to try them out? The outhouse out behind the church was perfect!

They all had a try at smoking and I'm sure that there was a good deal of coughing going on. Nobody liked it much! Then the bell rang. It was time for church, so they quickly threw their "weeds" away and ran in.

Shortly thereafter, somebody going to the outhouse discovered smoke rolling out of it!

The Montgomery Ward catalogue (which was the toilet paper in those days) was on fire!

The person who made the discovery quickly put out the fire, so no real harm was done, except that the outhouse seat was scorched a bit.

But what had started the fire?

Then it was remembered that Bobby and his buddies had been seen in the outhouse last.

When the preacher conducted an investigation and discovered what had taken place, believe me, there was one little preacher's son and his pals who also had scorched seats!

No "time out" business in those days! I happen to know that none of those boys ever smoked again, and are all following the straight and narrow path. Maybe there's something to be said for applied psychology!

Carol M. Hansen,
Coal Springs Church of God, Rural Meadow

ONE SUNDAY, MY MOM, CLARA, had pies baked and chicken in the oven when we went off to church. She had invited Effner and Stella Trapp and their family, Vernon, Duane and Lois, over for dinner after church. During the church service, Dick DeVaal, Mrs. Charlie Trapp's second husband, had to use the outdoor toilet. Dick, a big husky man, went outdoors, only to discover three men, supposedly bank robbers, siphoning gas out of the vehicles in the church parking lot. When he went to ask them what was going on, one of the men stuck a gun in his ribs, and they told him to get back into the church and start praying!

Later, when we returned home from church, my mom discovered that the robbers had also made a stop at our farm. They had stolen the freshly-baked pies and the chicken right out of the oven!

Arvel Trapp,
Grant Center Evangelical United Brethren Church,
Rural Milbank

HARRY, AGE FIVE, WAS A CITY BOY, and he and his parents were visiting friends in the country. So, on Sunday, they decided to go to church with their hosts. The preacher's sermon at the little rural church was from Acts, Chapter One, which talks about the Holy Ghost.

After the service, Harry's mom took him out back to the little house with the half moon on the door. Harry took one look at the little building and went screaming back to the church, refusing to go near the place.

They couldn't figure out what was the matter with him until he finally told them that he thought that's where that "Ghost" lived that the preacher had been talking about.

Carol M. Hansen,
Site and church unknown

Tests of Faith

OURS IS ONE OF ONLY A FEW continuing rural churches scattered across South Dakota. It is situated on a hill in a valley with beautiful trees and grounds. Years ago, the church building endured a tornado which moved it a quarter turn toward the south. The congregation members at the time figured that if God wanted it in that position, they would just leave it there! However, in 1949, a basement was built and the church was moved back to where it was originally.

Darlene Droz,
Pleasant Valley Community Church, Rural Miller

OURS WAS ONE OF THE FIRST CHURCHES built in Martin. The congregation of All Saints Episcopal Church grew steadily during the 1930's, as farmers moved into the new towns and businesses grew. By 1939, services were crowded with people, a choir had been organized, and a thriving club for high school boys made the church a center of social activity. People wished for a larger church, but with the country still mired deep in the Depression and Dust Bowl, local resources were inadequate to do any remodeling or expansion.

On July 19, 1939, my father, the priest, had called for a choir practice after supper and instructed Jimmy Weisbeck, one of the enthusiastic choirboys, to go round up the other boys and be back at the church at 7 p.m. Just as Jimmy was starting to leave, two men from Kyle arrived with a request that my father meet with them to do some church business. Knowing that their business would take a long time, my father then told Jimmy to contact the boys and tell them that choir practice would be cancelled. The sky in the west was starting to look very dark and ominous and my father didn't want the boys in church too late when a thunderstorm was coming.

Within a few minutes, the sky changed dramatically, and in the distance a large funnel cloud began to develop, touching down from time to time, but unquestionably headed for Martin at high speed. We rushed into the rectory as the wind began to increase, and my parents put my sister and me under the dining room table while the adults stood watching through the dining room window. The funnel touched down west of the schoolhouse two blocks away, and then immense winds hit the house. My father, the two men and my mother all braced themselves against the kitchen door to keep it from being blown down. I remember that several times the door came part-way open, but they always managed to close it.

Then one of the men looked over his shoulder and cried out "the church, the church." A strange glow and a calm break in the wind showed the church half-way off its foundations, rocking back and forth. Then the wind hit again and the church returned to its foundations, and then it rose dramatically, revealing the floor and joints. The church tilted back and forth a couple of times and then tipped completely over, just as the roof of the rectory tore loose, making an ungodly noise as nails that held it gave way. Then there was an eerie silence and a strange bright diffused light as everything settled.

Finally, we went outside. The theatre across the street from us was badly damaged and the cream station near it was almost completely flattened. We had to be careful getting out of the house and walking around in the debris because there were nails and glass all over the street. The brick Chevrolet garage down the alley west of us was completely gone, with a few bricks reminding us that there had been walls.

We stayed with friends that evening. The next day, as my father was standing on the ruined church steps, an old friend from college drove up. He was headed for the Black Hills and had just happened to pass through Martin. After viewing the wreckage, he told my father: "I'll be in touch again before Christmas." Then he drove off.

We used the Masonic lodge building for church services that fall, and just before the Christmas service, the friend called my father, saying that he had arranged a speaking tour of Ohio for my father to raise funds for another church. So my father toured Ohio in January and February of 1940, and with the money he raised and a contribution from St. John's Cathedral in Denver, St. Katherine's Episcopal Church and rectory was built that spring. With the new church, we gained six seats for the choir and doubled the congregation area. Some people remarked that the Lord is often very energetic when he wants to build new churches. We certainly can't deny that.

Vine Deloria, Jr.,
All Saints/St. Katherine's Episcopal, Martin

WHEN I WAS EIGHT YEARS OLD, during Thanksgiving week in 1930, our church burned down. My father, my mother, and my seven brothers and sisters and I had been to Strandburg to a Thanksgiving Service on Thursday evening. The next morning about 10 a.m., Edwin Dahlberg drove out to our farm to tell my parents the news, because we didn't have a telephone yet.

Of course, my dad raced into town right away to see what could be done. He found out that the fire had started about 2 a.m. in the morning. The Pastor, Rev. David Larson, lived in the parsonage right next to the church building. Fortunately, the pastor's home was not damaged. No one ever knew how the fire started, but perhaps the origin was electrical.

Only two things were saved from the fire. One was a small portable organ, which the pastor had taken home with him. The other was our silver communion service, which a deacon's wife had taken home to polish after the Thanksgiving service. Everything else in the building was destroyed.

There were only two churches in Strandburg, the Lutheran church at the south edge of town and our church at the north end. In this time of crisis, the Lutherans came to our rescue by letting us hold our services in their church building on Sunday afternoons. This arrangement went on for nearly two years.

I remember that when a house on the main street of Strandburg became empty in the summer, we rented it for Sunday school on Sunday mornings, and for our summer daily Vacation Bible School. Meanwhile, all of the people in the community donated materials and labor to help rebuild the church building. I was amazed to see this, as it was the 1930's and materials and money to rebuild were very scarce. The whole community, and people in nearby towns, pulled together to get the Baptists on their feet again.

Finally, in June of 1932, we were ready to move into our new building. The floor was not finished—we walked on boards laid diagonally and going into the corners. We had no pews yet, and sat on chairs borrowed from the American Legion Hall. Someone in the community had even donated a used piano to our congregation. We sang the old familiar hymns with joy and celebration in our voices that first Sunday! That was truly a service of Thanksgiving.

Helen Christenson,
Strandburg Baptist Church

THE RAVAGES OF A SUMMER STORM DESTROYED our small white rural church on August 12, 1999. Lightning struck the bell tower at about 6 a.m. The resulting fire nibbled the tower timbers until a farmer, toiling at his morning chores, noticed a strange ruddy glow in the sky beyond a nearby hill. He investigated, and finding the bell tower of the church ablaze, called the Langford Fire Department. While he watched, the bell tower tumbled to the ground. Fire departments from five nearby communities could not bring enough water to the scene to save the church. By 9:30 a.m., the white sentinel on the Day County Hill was burned to its foundation. Spectators at the site looked into the basement and saw in the rubble the metal frames of chairs sitting where the traditional Sunday fellowship hour had been enjoyed five days before.

The Rev. Craig Werling, co-pastor of the congregation with his wife, the Rev. Janine Rew-Werling, stated: "We are just thankful no one was hurt or killed." He reported that parishioners, determined to salvage something from the fire, had gone into the burning building and carried out the altar, the lectern, the baptismal font, a silver service, some parchments and church records.

The first Falnes Church, named in honor of Falnes Kirke, Norway, had opened for a service on Christmas Day in 1891, after seven years of labor and planning. On June 27, 1894, that building was destroyed by a tornado. Volunteer labor began building a second church immediately. The steeple was finished in 1895 and the chancel in 1897, and the dedication was held on February 16, 1898. In 1938 the church was renovated and moved from the center of the cemetery to its present location It was again remodeled and enlarged in 1948. The 100th anniversary of Falnes was celebrated in June, 1984.

A $27,000 remodeling project had been almost finished at the time of the 1999 fire. The 70-member congregation voted to rebuild again. A sister congregation, Highlanda, hosted the Falnes members during the interim period. Neighboring congregations gave funds, assisted with construction, held bake sales, and provided supplies for Falnes. The Royal Neighbors Camp No. 2500 gave a generous check to the rebuilding fund. Pews came from a vacated church in another town.

On Christmas Day, 1999, amid the aroma of fresh plaster and paint, service was held on the bare concrete floor of the new 36 by 76 foot chapel because the carpet had not arrived. The familiar altar and lectern, rescued from the burned church, were in place. A new piano would be delivered after the carpet installation. Clear window panes, without traditional trim, were temporary wind barriers while an area artisan prepared stained glass windows for the new sanctuary-fellowship hall.

This third Falnes Church building, beside a century-old cemetery, is again ready to host various community events and shelter the faithful.

Arvella Stokke,
Falnes Lutheran Church, Rural Day County

IT WAS IN NOVEMBER OF 1947. We lived about three blocks from the church and could see the fire and smoke. A young bride living near the church came to our place, as she was too frightened to be alone.

My husband was one of the men on the scene who tried to save some of the furnishings. The antique pulpit was carried out, but the fire spread so rapidly that further entrance was too dangerous. Yet they wanted to save the piano. A large strong man, a member of the congregation, was able to reach and get hold of the carpet. With his great strength and large hands, he pulled on the carpet and the piano came with it so the men could reach it and carry it to safety.

A church member, who lived on a nearby farm, saw the smoke and fire in town and could tell it was his church. He broke down and wept. It was thought that the fire was caused by an over-heated furnace.

Before another church building was purchased and moved to the site, the basement stood open, as it was very cold weather. No one remembered the large cistern standing open in the basement. What a frightening experience it was for parents to discover that two or three of their children were sliding on the ice on the cistern! No doubt it was well covered after that.

Meanwhile, the congregation held worship services in the basement auditorium of the Stockholm schoolhouse. Songbooks no longer used by another church were given to the group and congregation members continued worshipping God and giving out the Word until they again had a church building of their own.

Mauriece Southwick,
Elim Evangelical Covenant Church, Stockholm

A FIRE AT THE IONA CHURCH had burned it to the ground in the late 1960's. As far as the conference administrators were concerned, there was one less church in that district. The town of Iona itself was down to about seven souls. The church had outlasted even the pool hall and the beer joint, which means it was tougher than a boiled owl! But a fire took care of it; that is, until two of its members were having coffee at the filling station/store/emergency bread and milk place.

The two men looked out across the street where the church used to be. One of them said he missed seeing it there. The other commented that it was too bad it had burned down. Suddenly one said to the other: "Aw hell, you know, we could get a group together and rebuild it in a few days if we wanted to."

They soon rounded up a posse of people who brought their tractors and pay loaders and dug a hole. Another guy went into Gregory to get some cement block. Others brought all the tools necessary to do carpentry and electrical work. In a month they were ready to call the district superintendent and ask him to send them a preacher because they had rebuilt the church!

A dumbfounded district superintendent soon realized someone had slipped in the subversive activity of building a church while doing an end run around the District Committee on Building and Location! There had been no experts to do a community feasibility study or suggest models or architecture fitting the needs of the worshipers or go over "specs" for a pastor's study—nothing—nada! It was a church simply built in the image of two farmers' idea of what a church in Iona ought to look like. It is still there, a part of the Gregory-Iona parish.

Rev. Rod Gist,
Gregory-Iona Methodist Churches

COUNTRY CONGREGATIONS

On a summer day in 1883, homestead settlers of Pleasant Township, northeast of Willow Lake, gathered in Gulbrand Eggen's sod house to organize a church. They would call it the Norwegian Lutheran Church of Willow Lake. Rev. Olaf Hoil had come to get them started. It was the first organized church in Clark County, Dakota Territory.

They chose a cemetery spot on the top of a hill and knew they would build a church there some day. They continued to meet in homes until June of 1893, when they moved to their new church, which they had built beside the cemetery. They had also renamed it, after the township in which they lived.

The church was quite long, with five windows on each side. It had a very tall steeple and a bell. Every Sunday morning the bell rang and called people to worship. It was a good place where people worshiped God, brought their babies to be baptized, were confirmed, married and buried. They also had lots of good suppers where they served delicious food, hot, strong coffee and lefse.

Pleasant Church was the most important thing in the community for many years. It burned the afternoon of December 12, 1961, after a Christmas program practice. The children and teachers had gone home when the fire broke out. Firemen from the nearby towns could not save it. Most of the members joined the Vienna Lutheran Church.

On our field trip to Pleasant Cemetery, the birds were chirping, gophers were playing, the sun was shining and the wind was blowing through the tall trees. We stood on the hillside and could see far away. We saw the big bell, and markers giving information, but there was no church. Now all that is left is the cemetery. It is a good place.

Willow Lake 4th Grade Class/1999-2000,
Pleasant Norwegian Lutheran Church

For Richer, For Poorer

THE WEDDING SERVICE I recall the most was the one that had to be delayed a half hour because a herd of sheep was being moved. The bride lived across the street from the church and she was unable to get through the flock moving slowly down Main Street. The bride and groom who were married that day are still together after 70 years, so I guess it was worth the wait!

Pearl Lundquist,
Tabor Evangelical Lutheran Church, Strandburg

MY HUSBAND AND I WERE MARRIED in our little church. My father walked me down the aisle, the first of seven daughters for whom he would perform that traditional rite. He was so nervous at the wedding of his first daughter that, as we stood at the front of the church, he was stepping on the hem of my gown. I had to remind him several times to move his foot so I could join my husband-to-be at the altar. (He did much better at my sisters' weddings!)

Then, to my dismay, following our wedding reception, my new husband and I were paraded through the streets of town in a shiny new manure spreader. "Don't be upset, honey," he said. "It's just a local custom." I thought that they could have chosen a more suitable carriage, but at least it was shiny clean!

Shirley Reiners Conraads,
Twin Brooks Evangelical Church

IT WAS AN UNCOMMONLY HOT FRIDAY EVENING in June at Sinai Lutheran Church. We were sweating through rehearsal for my sister Jane's wedding. The minister's last words to the bridesmaids were: "Be sure to eat before the wedding—you girls diet a lot, and we don't want any fainting on this special occasion."

It was again very hot the next night. Heeding the minister's words, I filled my plate with barbequed pork in the church kitchen before the service. I had been dieting for weeks, but now my floral gown was a perfect fit.

Then the service began. Candelabras with 10 flames apiece framed the minister as he conducted the ceremony with a five-point message for the bride and groom. In the middle of Point Three, I began to lose my concentration. I noticed the minister turn toward the bridesmaids and mouth: "Set her down." I was only vaguely aware that the "her" was me. Strong arms grabbed me and guided me to a head-down position on the altar side chair. From the pastor's study door, an arm appeared with a glass of cool water. I lifted my head gratefully and sipped it. As I lowered my head again, hoping to overcome my dizziness, I heard my sister Kathie whisper: "Oh no, there goes Tom!"

I was horrified. What if it was my husband Tom? We would never live this down! I peeked through my fingers and saw that it was my brother Tom instead. Whew! This was bad, but it could have been much worse!

My brother was helped to the chair opposite mine, and we lowered our heads together, waiting patiently for the pastor to finish. After Point Five, we rejoined the bridal party at the altar. Then the ceremony ended and the beaming couple led us down the aisle. I'm certain that I heard people chuckling as I passed by on my husband's arm.

Poor Jane! To this day, when her wedding is spoken of, everyone remembers most vividly that her sister and brother fainted in the middle of it.

Sherry Larson DeBoer,
Sinai Lutheran Church

THERE WERE NO BIG WEDDINGS in our church in Strandburg during the lean 1930's and the war years. So in 1946, when the man I was going to marry was home safely from the war, I decided to have as big and beautiful a wedding as I could imagine and afford.

Arrangements seemed to go smoothly, and everything was set for September. But things do not always work out as planned. First, my father found out he had cancer that summer. But he insisted on getting up out of bed and walking me down the aisle. He did it well. (He died at Christmas time.)

The second problem that arose was in regard to flowers. The cost of a churchful of cut flowers from the Milbank florists was out of the question. My sister Ruth was teaching in a country school near Milbank. Her very kind landlady, Mrs. Jess Stengel, came forward to offer Ruth the flowers in her yard for my wedding. When we finished decorating the church, I thought I had never seen it look so beautiful.

Finally, the day of the big event came. Unfortunately, the county had torn up the road from LaBolt to Strandburg and it was nearly impassable. The only way we could get from our farm to town was by using our old Model A, which could navigate the ruts, mud, and dirt piles. On the day of my wedding, my brother, Arvid, had borrowed the car, promising to return it in plenty of time to get the family to my wedding. But of all the times for it to happen, his clock stopped and he was late picking us up.

Meanwhile, my sister Ruth, my bridesmaid, had developed a problem with the netting over her dress. Just minutes before the wedding was to start, my elder sister, Doris, was in the church vestibule, cutting and stitching the net so Ruth could walk down the aisle without tripping.

Meanwhile, my groom, Gordon, was pacing the church and wondering why I had jilted him at the altar!

Finally, the ceremony got started, and once underway, went without a further hitch. We have now been happily married for 55 years, and still laugh over the perils of the wedding that could have been a catastrophe.

Helen Christenson,
Strandburg Baptist Church

My wedding was on Saturday evening, June 3, 1944, in Fairview, South Dakota. That day, our pastor let me use the parlor in his parsonage home for changing and preparing, as our church next door had outdoor toilets and no private rooms.

But when the big moment for me to appear at the back of the church arrived, there was a downpour of rain. So, I changed back into my street clothes, covered my wedding clothes, and ran to the back door of the church and down into the basement. Because the church was filled with people, the only place for me to change again was behind the furnace. The problem was, the spider webs and dust back there hadn't been challenged for years!

Despite all of that, I did manage to get my wedding dress back on, hoping that my veil would cover my wet hair and that any clinging spider webs wouldn't show. Then I rushed up to the church entryway, where my father quickly took my arm, as the wedding music had already started. From then on, it was a wonderful occasion.

Miriam Loken Hardy,
Fairview Lutheran Church

In one of his weekly newspaper columns, our minister, Rev. F.W. Leyhe, wrote: "One incident always makes me smile whenever I think of it. It was during the hunting season. A young man went to Huron to get a marriage license. He applied for a license and the clerk of courts issued a hunting license for him. I asked for his license and he handed me the hunting license. I told him he could never get married on that! Well, he rushed over to Huron and exchanged the hunting license for a marriage license."

Alice Stegeman Mentzel,
St. John's Lutheran Church, Wolsey

"WHAT A BEAUTIFUL BOUQUET from Mrs. Garrett. I never expected to have one! Could this day be any happier for me?" This was Irene Hagny's response on her wedding day, August 19, 1934, when she was married to Les Swanson during the Sunday morning church service at their church.

The Rev. E. C. Beyer drove from Agar for the regular morning service. Immediately after he had delivered the sermon, Irene and Les and their attendants approached the altar. Irene was dressed in a white, lace-trimmed, street-length dress she had made for $5. She grasped the florist flowers, her unexpected gift from the church organist. The petite brunette wore her highest heels to stand beside her tall groom. Les was wearing the new suit he had purchased with money borrowed from his bride's father.

Irene and Les stood with their attendants, Clara Swanson and Bill Schmaltz. As was the custom at the time, the men of the congregation sat to the right of the center aisle, and the women and young children sat on the left. The vows this couple spoke on their wedding day sustained this marriage for 56 years, through sickness and health, through lean years and more prosperous ones.

Neither the simplicity of the wedding nor the economics of the Great Depression necessitated foregoing a wedding toast. The best man had a car, so after the church service and the many congratulatory good wishes, the four in the wedding party rode off to Forrest City, where Bill bought them each a beer.

After the wedding toast, the bridal party returned to the bride's family farm. Her mother and sisters had prepared for their extended families a huge Sunday noon "dinner" of chicken with all the trimmings and homemade pies.

On subsequent Sundays, the bride and groom returned to worship with their congregation in the little rural church. The special bond between them led to a change of tradition. Irene and Les and another progressive couple chose to worship side-by-side. Gradually the separation-of-sexes tradition was discontinued and entire families expressed their unity by worshipping together.

> Gladys Hagny,
> St John's Lutheran, Rural Agar

WHEN I WAS A GIRL, my Grandpa Harold Nelson would take my brothers and sisters and I for a ride to the Old Indian Church. The church was near his farm and he had played a key role in restoring and preserving the church grounds. Also, when I was a girl, I was told how my great-grandmother Emelia Johnson had attended church services at the Old Indian Church. She had traveled there by horse and worshiped while sitting on the earthen floor with the Sioux Indians. That log church has long been a favorite place of mine, which is why I chose it as the site for my wedding.

The details of that day remain vivid in my memory. The church was decorated with wreaths made of grapevines harvested from a nearby hollow. A bell was borrowed from a steam locomotive to ring at the wedding, as the church's bell had been taken from the steeple. A bouquet of wild prairie flowers arranged in an old oak basket rested on the bench near the entrance. Twin kerosene lamps with reflectors provided the light and a harpist from Sioux Falls provided music for the wedding ceremony, as the Old Indian Church had no electricity. The ring bearer carried a pillow I had sewn with a counted-cross stitch wreath of roses encircling our names and our rings. Outside the church, a black surrey with yellow fringe drawn by two white horses awaited to take us to the LaBolt Evangelical Covenant Church for the reception.

Pastor Dan Swanson and Father Larry Murtagh officiated at the ceremony. Attending me were my three sisters, Nancy Seaquist, Carolyn Hartleip, and Vicki Stewart. Rachel Larson was the flower girl. Attending my husband-to-be, Daniel Carl Dombrowski, were his two brothers, David and Randy Dombrowski, and a boyhood friend, Rob Tomasek. Jeremy Stewart was the ring bearer. Mark Seaquist, my brother-in-law, sang two solos accompanied by the harp.

I remember standing outside at the church's entrance, after the rest of the wedding party had proceeded to the front of the church. The wedding march was being played on the harp. I paused for a moment, leaned nearer my dad, and whispered, "Let's walk very slow." I wanted to cherish the moment, the place, and the people.

On our wedding day, we were blessed with the presence of family and many friends. Our parents, Cecil and Joyce Larson of LaBolt and Norbert and Gloria Dombrowski of Phoenix, Arizona, my two grandmothers, all six of my brothers and sisters with their families, and my husband's two brothers were in attendance.

One of my favorite keepsakes of that day is a photograph. Everyone attending the wedding gathered on the south side of the Old Indian Church for a picture. Looking back at that photograph, I see many family members and friends who have since passed away, including my Grandma Agnes Nelson. My Grandma Nelson often told me stories when I was young, and my favorites always began with her saying "When I was a girl..." When I was a girl, the Old Indian Church was one of my favorite places, and it still is.

Valerie Dombrowski,
Old Indian Church, Rural Stockholm

Coming Forward

THE LADIES IN OUR CHURCH generally wore scarves in the early days, and kept their heads covered to attend mass. My mother Stella Konechne had a large family and no luxuries, but one year she decided that she wanted a hat for Easter. So, she saved money for a long time from selling eggs and bought a hat that she really admired for 98 cents. Then she had terrible feelings of guilt, because she was used to giving to her family and to the church, and not to herself.

On Easter Sunday, our family all piled into the buggy, proud of our mother in her new hat. Down the road the buggy went, where a nasty gust of wind grabbed my mother's hat and sent it flying down the road. It was retrieved, but in very poor condition. My mother was convinced that she had been punished for being selfish and returned to wearing her scarf, vowing never to be so vain again.

Lucille Houda,
Holy Trinity Church, Bendon (relocated to Kimball in 1982)

EARLY CHURCH WOMEN SERVED IN MANY CAPACITIES. Pioneers who migrated from Scandinavian countries were not accustomed to supporting a church financially, because the state churches in their native lands were subsidized by governments. Women, especially, responded to this new financial dilemma. They manipulated knitting needles, crochet hooks, embroidery supplies and antique sewing machines to create saleable items. Profits from these time-consuming efforts were often used to help pay pastors' salaries, build or repair churches, and purchase equipment.

Despite such laudable efforts by women, however, in many pioneer churches, only men voted in business meetings. Even the first president of the Ladies' Aid in Blom Lutheran Church, rural Sinai, was a man, Nils Svaren, who was skilled as a tailor.

In one frontier church, an especially conscientious woman served as treasurer of the Ladies' Aid. She took her responsibility so seriously that she asked her son to dig a hole in their sod house floor. Carefully, she placed her cigar box of Aid money in the hole for safekeeping. When her term expired, she refused re-election. She considered it too awesome a responsibility.

Also, although this story cannot be documented, it is worth sharing. A dedicated Ladies' Aid treasurer hurried to the local bank. She told the employee in broken English, "I'd like to deposit Aid money." The innocent teller thought she said "egg" money. So she replied: "The old hens are doing well."

Before church buildings were constructed, worship services were held in homes, so women also spent much time preparing their primitive living quarters for services. Yes, women played major roles in early country church life.

Helen J. Svaren,
Trinity Lutheran Church, Arlington

ONE PROMINENT CHARACTERISTIC of the small rural church I attended as a child was the adherence to traditions. For example, during the first hour on Sunday mornings, the men always stayed outside, in the cool shade on the west side of the building in the summer or in the meager warmth of their cars in winter, while the women accompanied the children inside for Sunday school. Also, the men always exited directly after the service, while the women gathered in the small entry hall to visit.

And, most important of all, the men always sat on the left side of the aisle, and the women always sat on the right during the service. The children stayed at the front where they had gathered for their Sunday school classes.

Then, one Sunday, when I was still a member of the "front of the church" group, that last tradition was broken, to the shock of all present.

A college student, the daughter of one of the church families, returned for a weekend visit, accompanied by her fiancé. She marched right down the aisle and sat with her fiancé on the men's side of the church! All eyes turned in her direction. All the men looked very uncomfortable. The women on their "proper" side of the church stifled gasps. We children wondered how that young woman had the courage to challenge the tradition, and we waited anxiously for the next Sunday to see if a new tradition had begun.

But, of course, it hadn't. The next Sunday morning, everyone was "properly," and separately, in place. Not until our little country church merged with its sister churches in the small town nearby did the tradition fade.

Marilyn Kratz,
Neuberg Congregational Church, Rural Scotland

AS A YOUNG GIRL, I loved going to the annual Montrose Catholic Church supper. It was a feast! Mounds of thickly sliced ham, creamy mashed potatoes and gravy, and the most delicious sour cream and raisin, pumpkin, and cherry pies adorned the tables.

The women did all of the work: the chopping, the peeling of potatoes, the baking, the serving. My tiny Aunt Kathryn Gill was in the kitchen lifting huge pots from one stove to another. She ran the show.

Fast forward 30 years! I took my friends Si Rogers and Fernie Erskine for a return to the feast. Was this the same event? Men were in the kitchen peeling potatoes, lifting roasters of ham and washing dishes. Some pies were homemade and disappeared quickly. Some were store-bought too. I doubt that any of the ladies of 30 years ago would have showed up with store-bought pies.

Rebecca Dunn,
Montrose Catholic Church

"Honey, come look at this!" my husband called to me one very early morning when he flipped on the outdoor light and opened up the front door of our new home in a quiet country town. Climbing up the steps was a huge salamander, black with orange-yellow markings like licks of flame.

"Don't salamanders usually stay away from light?" my husband asked.

I knelt and bent forward, leaning on my hands and knees close enough to look right into its eyes, and still the creature remained steadfastly on the step, bathed in the porch light. I was reminded of a dictionary description I had read recently: "Salamander: 2. A mythical lizard or other creature fabled to withstand fire."

"Now it's time for you to go home," I whispered fiercely. "The light from the door is only a shadow."

Slowly, the salamander turned its prehistoric head, arcing its gaze over its opposite shoulder to the black silhouettes of grass surrounding the house, then brought its face back to mine. At that moment, oddly, what I saw in the salamander's eyes made me think of what could have been in Jesus' gaze toward the strange light shroud over Jerusalem as He was tested in the desert, what could only have been the light of God, which saved Him from evil, the same great light which offered salvation to all people in darkness, the light written of in Matthew 4:16.

I deeply felt an understanding between the salamander and me, a connection between our journeys, one spiritual, the other instinctual. In fact, I felt suddenly that we had exchanged those journeys, and that the salamander was suddenly the kneeling woman on the porch step, and I was the salamander gazing up at her. Then, what my salamander's heart knew of the woman was this: she was a woman on a spiritual journey who had traveled through a filigree of wilderness, and had come to a place of vast fire, with no passage but through the flames, those flames which were now casting that same strange saving light on our paths.

In the rooms of my salamander mind, the recesses of my amphibian knowledge of "In the Beginning...," I knew this woman who bound herself to me in the shadow of the border between light and dark, her heart illumined by the strange light of fire she had failed to recognize until she had taken herself out of her familiar church home into the incredible aloneness of spiritual exile.

Eighteen months earlier, this woman had left her parish in another town, in the wake of what she considered to be a betrayal of women. The new young priest had refused to have a Sister for the parish; he felt that "most Sisters" were "way off-base theologically." Congruently, the same priest had ignored her request that he pray with her family for her troubled teenage daughter.

Then the salamander and I repeated our exchange of journey and spirit. Once again the woman I know as myself, I watched the salamander get back on its path. "Thank you," I whispered to the sighing of amphibian feet which faded into the wilderness of long grass.

I returned to Mass that Sunday, bringing my three youngest children with me to the church in our new hometown. After the service, I was overwhelmed with the women, young and old, who advanced on me, a wave of love welcoming me with hugs and blessings. In their eyes, I saw that they recognized me as one of their own who could withstand fire.

> Evie L. Rice,
> St. Anthony's Catholic Church, Selby

IT WAS MY TURN TO CLEAN THE CHURCH. In the process I often prepared a vase of flowers for the altar. On Saturday, my husband and I were riding along the country road and I spied these tall beautiful cattails, just what I needed, as my flower bed was about depleted. "Stop, I cried, "look at those beautiful cattails!" So my husband got out of the car and with his trusty jackknife cut me a beautiful bouquet with long stems. "I picked the green ones," he said. So we motored on, I happily imagining how the cattails would look on the altar. On Saturday evening, I went over to the church and sat them to one side of the altar in a tall gold vase.

On Sunday morning, I felt like everything was in order. My oldest daughter and I arrived at the church early and she helped me carry in my Sunday School materials. As I walked to the altar, for a second I was petrified. My beautiful bouquet of cattails! Half of them had burst! The soft fuzzy seeds covered the carpet front of the altar! "Quick," I said, turning to my daughter, "get the vacuum!" I grabbed a waste basket, and we quickly cleaned up the mess as best we could. I did save a few that still looked sound and said a silent prayer that they would last through the service, and they did.

Bessie Brozik,
Dixon Baptist Church

"GRACE" IS ONE OF THE MOST SIGNIFICANT WORDS in any understanding of Christian theology. It represents the generous and unexpected blessings bestowed on us by a loving God.

"Grace" is also a woman's name.

The two meanings came together in a special way for the members of our church, in the person of Grace Wilkins.

Grace was a member of the church for about 70 years, until her death in 1997. She will be long remembered by many of us, especially when we sing, "Amazing Grace."

It all started one Sunday during the morning service, in Grace's 87th year. As we were singing, Grace fainted! There was a flurry of activity in her pew as those sitting next to her assessed the situation and tried to determine what to do. I stopped the singing and went quickly to where she was. We laid her out on the pew, one woman fanning her face, another raising her feet above her head, and a third taking her pulse. One of the ushers ran up the block to the Presbyterian Reformed Church, where he knew the town ambulance driver was at worship.

It was only a matter of a minute or two when Grace, much to the relief of a rather stunned congregation, came to. By that time, the ambulance driver and an assistant had stormed in the door with the usher. As Grace slowly sat up, the color returned to her face. When asked if she wanted the ambulance, she strongly protested. When asked how she would get home, she insisted she would drive. As she left the church with a friend who would see her home, she turned to the congregation and quipped, "Don't worry, I'm not dead yet!" Laughing and smiling, we returned to the hymn we had been singing, "Amazing Grace."

This was the first time Grace fainted in church. It wouldn't be the last. On several Sunday mornings over the next 18 months, Grace fainted, and we all responded. We got to the point where we all knew our roles; head down, feet up, take the pulse, fan the face. But we didn't go for the ambulance driver after the first time. We knew she wouldn't stand for that again.

And every time Grace fainted, frail woman that she was, I wondered silently, "will she come out of this one?" It was almost like she knew her time was approaching and she couldn't think of a better time or place to lay her life down.

My response to the situation changed from one of fear and powerlessness the first time it happened to one of faith and confidence after that. Before long, it was OK with me if she died in our midst.

Amazing Grace, how sweet the sound, that helped the blind to see.

Rev. Carl Kline,
United Church of Christ, Willow Lake

I REMEMBER ESPECIALLY A FUNERAL I conducted for a very elderly Lakota woman. After the service at the little white wood church and burial in the cemetery beside it, her husband and family invited everyone present to a feast in her honor.

When we arrived at the couple's home, I was astounded. It was absolutely empty, except for the feast food. I knew immediately what had happened because I'd heard of this custom from tribal elders, although I'd never witnessed it before.

The woman's husband, to show how much he loved her, had given away everything. Nothing he could have said would have been as eloquent as that barren house. It was clear that she was more valuable to him than anything he possessed, and that without her, he had nothing.

Father Fred Jessett,
St. Andrew's Episcopal Church, Spring Creek

What Was Is

IN 1978, AMERICA FINALLY REALIZED that freedom of religion was for all Americans and enacted the American Indian Religious Freedom Act. Until the late 1960's, the Christian churches and the government had driven our sacred Lakota ceremonies underground. The Lakota Nation had been forced to practice its beliefs secretively. Debasing books were written and inappropriate photographs were taken of these covert ceremonies. The passage of the Act meant that we would finally be able to conduct our sacred ceremonies openly, respectfully and authentically. It seemed we had to step backward in time to recover what we had lost.

The assimilation policies had failed, yet the people had become divided by the churches and the government. Fear of incarceration and other punishment and fear of ridicule had smothered the will of many to participate in our sacred ceremonies over the years. People had turned tightly within themselves, like cocoons, and had masked their faces into obsidian shadows when Lakota ceremonies were mentioned. Some even denied their Lakota heritage and claimed to be more French than Lakota and ridiculed the darker people, calling them "buck Indians" or "bucky." Many still whispered stories of priests and ministers breaking into homes, destroying sacred items, and calling our ceremonies "devil worship." People were harassed and condemned. They were even told they would not be buried with their families if they continued attending Lakota ceremonies. To a nation of people whose entire philosophy is based on kinship, a nation without a concept of "Hell," imagining this separation was hell. We felt our spirits were collapsing inward.

We knew that the wounds and division among the people would take many years to heal. But we were determined to tell our sacred stories to the younger generations. Gradually, like a bear coming out of a long winter of hibernation, the ceremonies came out into the open, cautiously waiting for a suffocating reaction. Some thought maybe a trickster's grin hid behind that non-malignant Act, but ceremonies like the inipi, the purification ceremony with its sweet scent of cedar and sage, began to lift us from anger and bitterness.

On the first day of the official return of the Sundance, the dancers stood facing east as the sun came over the horizon. They held bouquets of sage in front of their faces and wept as they prayed. A woman led them, carrying a pipe representing the White Buffalo Calf Woman who had brought our way of life to us. The men, mostly veterans who had fought to defend this country, followed the woman into the arbor. Dressed in Sundance shirts of many colors, they carried symbols of all nations: the four-legged, the buffalo, the elk and deer; the winged nations, the eagle, the owl, the singing birds, the dragonfly and the butterfly; and the crawling nations. The cedar and sage they carried represented the plant nations. The women followed, weeping, wearing cloth and buckskin dresses, sage crowning their unfurled hair. Many were Gold Star mothers who had given their sons to this nation's wars. Each dancer held a pipe tightly to his heart, the pipe which had carried our Lakota, Dakota and Nakota Nations through the genocide, the attempts at ethnic cleansing.

This was a tenuous time. The piercing sounds of eagle bone whistles and ceremonial song came together with the wind as one spirit as the people prayed. Even after the drums echoed into the valley, into the evening glow, in the hushed silence of the arbor, there were tears, tears of joys and sorrow. Tears for the freedom to pray as our ancestors had once prayed. Tears for all those who had gone on, and for those who had been persecuted, jailed and ridiculed and who were still determined to preserve our beliefs.

The dancers finished each day feeling spiritually stronger. After the fourth sunrise, the ache that filled us seemed to grow weaker. We knew that our nation would go on but that it would take time for us to recover from the century of persecution. Our ceremonies had strengthened us to endure. We had persevered because of the strength of our elders and because of our values of Wowacintanka, fortitude, Woohitika, bravery, Wacantognaka, generosity, and Woksape, wisdom.

We do not have a Lakota word for religion. Tunkasila (God, Grandfather) is in Tate (the wind), in Magajukiya (each fresh raindrop), and in each sunrise and sunset. Tunkasila is in the first breath of a newborn, and in Unci's (Grandmother's) last sigh. It is in Tunwin's (Aunt's) comforting words. It is in LaLa's (Grandfather's) and Leksi's (Uncle's) wise counsel. It is in a smile, in our laughter and in our tears. Tunkasila is truly a part of us and of all of creation. It is Mitakuye Oyasin, for we are all related to all of creation. One word cannot describe this beautiful concept.

It is beyond words. It is beyond imagination. It is all around us. How could one look at creation and not think of God? It is Lakolwicoun. It is a way of life.

This was the first Sundance held by the Sicangu since the Sundance was declared illegal. The first women who came out to dance are called Sundance Mothers. In this renewed beginning, only one Sundance song was remembered and that one song was sung that entire day. Yet, the spirit of that one song joined with the sky and the earth, and with each sacred direction, to bring to us hope. Each offering, each sacrifice, each color, the cottonwood tree and the star that connects us all and that one song, were sent out to the universe, to the infinite power of Tunkasila.

Tunkasila did answer the prayers of that first Sundance. As the years passed, songs that had been disguised as lullabies and sung to children at night joined the ceremonies. The bond with the Mystery was strengthened. Yes, times change, yet the spirit of the Creator and the people live on.

Maybe—just maybe—the war against us has finally come to an end.

SUNDANCE SONG

Wakan Tanka, Tunkasila	Great Mystery, Grandfather
Pilamayayelo yehe	I thank you
Canupa Wakan ca	(for) this sacred pipe
Mayaku yelo heye	you have given me
Pila mayayelo heye	I thank you
Wacozani wan mayaku welo	(for) Health (spiritual and physical), You have given me
pilamayaye,	I thank you
pilamayayelo heye	I thank you

Lydia Whirlwind Soldier,
Rosebud

Becoming History

RISING AS IT DID—AND DOES—from the McCook County prairie, our church served the largely German farm families living between Canova and Salem. Its white siding gleamed above its flat surroundings, and although the trees straggling to the south of the building have softened its appearance, the old cemetery nestled against its side has provided an ageless reminder of time's passing. The gravestones chronicling the lives and deaths of the founding generation, including my great-grandfather, and identifying the victims of the flu epidemic of 1918, have inspired countless trivia games: "Now, if Herman was Emil's grandfather, how was he related to John and Emily?"

My own family history—both sides of my father's family, in fact—has found silent expression on the slightly slanting slabs of marble or on softer, disintegrating limestone. As a boy, I mowed the church yard, including the cemetery, and was always strangely moved by the triple tombstone marking the resting places of Grandpa Marten's three young siblings, who had died within days of one another early in the century.

James Marten,
Immanuel Lutheran Church, Canova

MANY TRADITIONS HAVE BEEN HELD onto by our little church in the valley. Most of the graves are dug by hand. In fact, some members make it known that they would like fellow members to dig their graves. Younger members regard this as an honor because it is the last human thing that can be done for the deceased member. One particular member keeps a special spade sharpened for this task. There is much camaraderie and fellowship that goes on at the grave-digging. Once, as they were working hard with their spades, one of the men commented, "When you dig my grave, dig it so my head is about six inches higher than my feet."

Marvin and Alma Lau,
Herb and Janett Uttecht,
St. Peter Lutheran Church, Rural Armour

THE CHURCH OF MY CHILDHOOD now sits unused on the prairie, west of Platte. It closed about 20 years ago but is maintained by nearby farmers, who preserve the building and the adjoining graveyard. It looks much the same as when it was built over 100 years ago. Even the two weather-beaten outhouses in back are still there and functional. The white building, with tin-covered steeple pointing skyward, now stands only as a symbol of those days when Sunday services were held and hundreds of baptisms, weddings, and funerals were performed.

Although the church is now empty, its doors are never locked. I live out-of-state, but when I return "home," I always worship at my church. I enter with reverence, sit in the pew where my family always sat, and allow memories to flood my thoughts. It is truly a worship experience, with both spiritual and personal significance.

The small graveyard on the south side of the church is filled with my family members. My great-grandparents are in the back left corner, near the grain field. My grandparents are near the center, close to the church, and my parents are near the front. Around them are scores of uncles, aunts, and cousins. They all now rest quietly together in a permanent family reunion.

Although I often worship in the church alone, I never feel alone. I feel a part of a large congregation, even though most of that congregation now sleeps in the graveyard by the side of the church. I feel they are all with me, as I sit in silence with my memories. I never leave without offering a prayer of thanks for my spiritual and family heritage. Those experiences remind me that the influence of a church does not stop when it closes its doors. Things that are spiritual are not just preached from pulpits. Worship can occur as you sit silently in thought and prayer.

This old country church still serves its community well. Its role is different, but no less meaningful than when it was active those many years ago.

Marvin A. Johnson,
Trinity Lutheran Church, Rural Platte

GROWING UP IN A COUNTRY CHURCH was a pleasure and an inspiration. Our little community had three churches, a school, a town hall and a country store during my growing up years. The church not only met our spiritual needs, but our social needs as well. We attended potluck suppers, Bible studies, youth groups, Bible school, weddings, funerals, and christenings.

Our country church is truly a treasure in my memory. It paralleled our way of life. We were a farming community, and the church emphasized the cycle of the seasons. I especially loved the Harvest Festival. Every fall, an evening was set aside where each family was to bring something of the harvest to the altar. It could be canned goods, pumpkins, squash, corn, sheaves of wheat, or whatever else was reminiscent of the harvest. In my child's view, the most memorable moments were the potluck supper and the singing of favorite hymns. I can still see the faces of those faithful, work-worn stewards of the land singing praises to their God.

One of my favorite hymns, "The Church in the Wildwood" says it best. "No Place is so dear to my childhood as the little brown church in the vale." Our country church wasn't brown but a brilliant white, and it shines like a jewel in my memory.

Jan Brozik Cerney,
First Baptist Church, Dixon

A Meaningful Goodbye

THOSE WHO ATTENDED THAT LAST SERVICE knew the evening would be emotional and memorable. But little did we realize how much it would mean in later years.

Have you ever driven around where you grew up, and thought of the buildings and homes that are no longer present? It's an unsettling feeling for those of us with cherished memories. You want things to still be there. But they aren't. Maybe it wouldn't seem so hard to accept if you had been there when the removal occurred. But now all you know is that something is missing. You try to remember exactly where your favorite building was located. In your mind's eye, you do your best to resurrect the facility, but you just can't seem to get it right.

Well, that night in the old United Methodist Church in Faith, Christians came together to say goodbye to an old church that had seen better days. A new church was in the works and the old parsonage and church had to come down. This was the final ceremony. The church would be razed the next day. There was singing, a grand sermon by Pastor Bruchlacher, and finally, at the end of the service, people formed a circle around the outer walls of the church, joined hands, and shared stories.

There were remembrances of weddings, funerals, concerts, church basement prayer meetings and community events. We laughed and we cried as people shared their stories. Everyone was invited to participate. Catholics, Lutherans, Methodists—all had stories to tell.

It was a meaningful goodbye to a rural country church on the South Dakota prairie. And now when those of us who attended that last service drive by the beautiful new church, there are no negative feelings, only wonderful memories of the church that was and will always be.

Linda Hipps,
United Methodist Church, Faith

Suggestions for Further Research, Thought and Discussion

1. Learn more about traditional Native American religion through library research. If possible, discuss that religion with a knowledgeable tribal person.

2. Examine the history of your county to learn more about the early churches in your area. Find their locations, and visit the ones that remain. Visit a rural church that has been restored.

3. Attend a rural church service, and visit with the leaders and the parishioners. Write a narrative of your experience.

4. Consider the differences between traditional Native American religion and Christianity, and the differences between Christian denominations. Consider the similarities.

5. Through library research, learn of the religious traditions of more recent immigrants, such as Muslims and Buddhists, which are not Christian or Native American. Again, consider differences and similarities.

6. Write a paper about all of the religious traditions of the region, briefly explaining what can be learned from each of them, and what can be learned from studying the region's history of religious experience.

SOURCES CONSULTED AND SUGGESTED READINGS

Berry, Thomas. *The Dream of the Earth*. San Francisco: Sierra Club Books, 1988.

Eastman, Charles Alexander (Ohiyesa). *The Soul of the Indian*. Lincoln and London: University of Nebraska Press, First Bison Book printing, 1980.

Grobsmith, Elizabeth S. *Lakota of the Rosebud: A Contemporary Ethnography*. Fort Worth, Chicago, et al., 1981.

Hartill, Lane. "From City to Soil," *Christian Science Monitor*, November 7, 2001, pp. 12-13.

Ostergren, Robert C. "The Immigrant Church as a Symbol of Community and Place in the Upper Midwest," *Great Plains Quarterly*, Vol. 1, No. 4, Fall, 1981, pp. 224-238.

Ostergren, Robert C. "European Settlement and Ethnicity Patterns on the Agricultural Frontiers of South Dakota," *South Dakota History*, Spring/Summer, 1983, Vol. 13, Nos. 1 and 2, pp. 49-82.

Parker, Donald Dean. *Founding the Church in South Dakota*. Brookings: South Dakota State College History Department, 1962.

Shepard, Paul. "Place in American Culture," *The North American Review*, Fall, 1977, Vol. 262, No. 3, pp. 22-32.

Sneve, Virginia Driving Hawk. *Completing the Circle*. Lincoln: University of Nebraska Press, 1995.